SHORT STORIES FOR THE MANAGER

Sunil Thomas, Ph.D.

SUNIPRINT

A Division of Abraham Thomas Foundation

SHORT STORIES FOR THE MANAGER

Cover Design: Sunil Thomas

ISBN: 978-1-7337488-5-8

SUNIPRINT
A Division of Abraham Thomas Foundation
11 Cambridge Road, Broomall, PA-19008,
USA.
E-mail: suniprintbooks@gmail.com

CONTENTS

I

II

PREFACE

Leaders are people who do the right thing, managers are people who do things right. – Warren Bennis

Everyone is a manager. You do not need a title or education to be a manager.

When you are born, your parents manage for you. They clean you, dress you up, provide food and also put you to sleep. Eventually you take over and manage yourself. Management starts with you. What you think you will become. Everyone manage themselves differently. Avoiding smoking, having a healthy diet, educating yourself, dressing up elegantly, are all good self-management principles. People are living longer than the previous generations due to better medicine, advanced technology, education, access to food and improved lifestyle. Good management principles are required for personal and professional growth.

A person who is of age 80 years will have lived through four generations. Whatever the person had seen in his childhood will be obsolete by the time he or she turns 80. The culture, technology, people, climate and even the city or country you live may have changed in these years. To be successful to live up to 80, one must knowingly or unknowingly be a good manager. Remember, very few private organizations managed by professional managers survive 80 years.

1

Every person has hundreds of stories in their life that build them and made them who they are. However, most people do not recognize their stories because they do not pay attention. This book 'Short Stories for the Manager' are stories from my life or people I know. The stories could help you find the manager in you and also help you to be a great manager.

Sunil Thomas

1. HONESTY

One of my favorite stories during my school days was about the woodcutter and the river goddess. Briefly, the river goddess gifted the wood cutter with a golden and silver axe for his honesty, whereas she punished the wood cutter's greedy neighbor for his dishonesty.

The quiz competition (questions on general knowledge) is a favorite literary competition since the 1970s. Once there was a quiz competition conducted by a children's magazine during my Middle School years. I prepared very well for the competition. The quiz master would ask the questions and we had to write it on the answer sheet. The prize would be given to the student with the highest score.

After the quiz competition, the answer sheets were evaluated. The first prize was announced. I was surprised, I was the winner! I walked and stood on the dais behind the editor of the children's magazine. Subsequently, the other prizes were announced.

When I stood on the dais, I saw a wad of the answer sheet in the quiz master's hand. My eyes fell on the answer sheet below.

Once the announcement was over, I asked the quiz master if I could see my answer sheet. "Of course," replied the quiz master. He showed me the winning answer sheet. I glanced at the answer sheet and said, "It is not mine; it is my classmate's answer sheet. We have the same name. You missed the family name at the end of his name." The quiz master apologized and the new winner was announced.

Be honest, never cheat. There is always a temptation to cheat others, especially when you think that nobody is watching. Honesty and integrity are the important qualities of great leadership in business.

2. DAILY BREAD

Everyone is aware of the Lord's Prayer: Our Father, who art in heaven, hallowed be thy name; thy kingdom come; thy will be done on earth as it is in heaven. Give us this day our daily bread; and forgive us our trespasses as we forgive those who trespass against us; and lead us not into temptation, but deliver us from evil. Amen.

Decades back our neighbor had a large mango tree in front of his house. Some of the branches extended into our property. The neighbor's house was vacant; however, occasionally he came to clean his house.

One summer, the tree was full of mangoes. By May, the mangoes turned ripe. My siblings (brother and sister) asked if I could get some mangoes. I plucked a couple of mangoes and gave them. They asked for more. I said, "The scriptures say…give us this day our daily bread….I will get more mangoes tomorrow."

The next day, when I reached home from school my siblings were fuming pointing to the mango tree. Apparently, the neighbor came and harvested all the mangoes leaving nothing on the tree.

They asked in unison, "Where is my daily bread…the mango. Some sort of Messiah."

5

I said, "The scriptures also state…Thy shall not covet your neighbor's property."

Anyway, to cool down the situation, I got some mangoes from the grocery store.

Opportunities don't last forever.

3. THE FULL CIRCLE

My initial education was at our family home. As with every people, my mother was my first teacher. The parapet of the portico was the "table" where I started learning to read and write. Several months into my initial education, my father moved to the neighboring State and we also followed him. After more than two decades, my parents came back and re-settled at our ancestral family home. Around that time, I completed my Ph.D.

After completing my Ph.D thesis, I placed a copy of the thesis in a leather bag and brought home. I asked my parents to sit on the parapet of the portico, the same place I started my education. I gave the leather bag to my parents and asked to open the bag. The moment my parents opened the leather bag was the "Ph.D thesis release." My formal education was over.

The best thing in life are moments. Sometimes you have to create moments that everyone cherish.

4. THE HOSTEL WARDEN: MS. OLGA MIRANDA

Ms. Olga Miranda was the warden of our boarding school. There were around forty boys in the boarding. The beds were all kept clean and tidy. Every weekend Ms. Miranda would check our suitcases to see whether the clothes were arranged properly. Since Ms. Miranda did not trust us, she would take out the clothes above and see if the clothes below were folded and arranged well. She would also see that everyone would polish their shoes before leaving the boarding hall to their classes. Anyone who do not follow the "laws" would be in the "firing range." Literally.

Every morning we would wake up at 5:30 and go the school chapel in a line. Ms. Miranda was also very generous with us. On Sundays, before going to the school chapel, she would provide money from her purse to the first five students for the church offering. The following week it would be the next five students. After many years of stellar service to the boarding school Ms. Miranda moved out when she was offered a job near her home.

It was chaos at the boarding school after Ms. Miranda left. The next warden, Ms. Mary, was not very effective in managing the boarding school. She had a large cane to control the boys. One day some of the boys took a decision,

"We should hide the cane." Within a week the cane disappeared, and we could see Ms. Mary looking out at every nook and corner of the dormitory for her cane. Since it was a top secret, none of us knew who hid the large cane. Anyway, it provided some relief to the students. A couple of months later, I completed elementary education and moved to a new school.

Not everyone is effective in running an organization.

5. KEEP MOVING, EVEN IF YOU DON'T SEE THE WAY

When I was a child, summer holidays was fun. The boarding school was closed, and we could spend time at our estate. It would be merrier when our relatives and cousins would also join us.

Behind our house was a hill covered with tall grass. There was a narrow trail to get to the top of the hill. However, the tall vegetation would obscure the trail during some days, especially when it was windy. A keen eye was required to find the trail to reach the top of the hill.

One day after breakfast, my father said he had some urgent work to complete before noon. After he left, my uncle said, "Why don't we go to the top of the hill?" My cousins were excited.

"Good idea."

Once we started ascending the hill from the base, we got lost. We had no idea where the trail was. It was tall grass everywhere.

My uncle said, "Keep moving even if you don't see the trail." Once we reached three quarters of the hill, we saw at a distance the cattleman herding the cattle after forage.

We shouted to the cattleman, "Where is the trail?"

From a distance he pointed the trail with his long stick.

Everyone was happy on reaching the trail after walking among the tall grass.

Sometimes in life we don't see what is ahead of us. Keep moving.

6. A HEAVY PRICE FOR HONESTY

In our school there was a day in a year where students run the school. The students would replace the teachers and teach in every class. Students were also assigned to take the role of principal and vice principal.

I just started high school. A student was assigned to teach history in our class. He was not fully prepared; he was repeating the same page of the book. When I gazed outside the text book, I saw students in the last row reading comic books placed inside the text books! As I was bored hearing the same lesson repeatedly, I asked my bench mate for a comic book. He communicated my message softly across the class and several minutes later I had the comic book. Bad luck; someone noticed from the neighboring building that I was reading a comic book and reported.

The following day the class teacher angrily came to the class; he was also the physical training teacher of the school. He was angry and frustrated that his class had the reputation of being the worst class that year. He knew me very well and was confident that I did not bring the comic books from home. He asked me, "Did you read the comic book. If so, who gave you? If you admit it, I will give you three spankings, if you don't provide the names, you will be given three more."

I replied, "I read the comic book, but I do not know whose book it was."

I received six spankings with his cane for my honesty.

A couple of weeks later the principal saw me. He asked me to bring my parents to see him. I did not take his words seriously. However, several weeks later my parents said, "We want to see how you are doing at school, we will be coming to school today." My heart raced. I imagined all the worse scenario.

My parents came when the school assembly was in progress. The band played the national anthem during the assembly. For the first time in the history of the school, the band made a mistake while playing the national anthem (the incident seemed like the parting of the Red Sea by Moses). The principal was angry and furious. He blamed the teachers for not training the students well. (The teachers revolted against the principal the following year).

After the school assembly was over, my parents went to the principal's office. He was still fuming from the national anthem debacle. He discussed with my parents about the inferior quality of his teachers!

Had the national anthem debacle did not happen, the principal could have stated about me reading the comic book in class. My parents were strict. I would have been asked to quit school forever! Looked like someone up wished to see me educated and preferred me over to the school.

The following year, our class was selected one of the best class of the school. I completed my tenth grade with distinction and enrolled at a nearby junior college.

On the last day of my junior college, a former classmate from my school approached me. He stated sheepishly, "I was the one who betrayed you in school. I saw you reading the comic book in high school several years back and I informed the authorities. I am sorry."

Be honest, even if you lose your head; someone above is watching you.

7. THE CHAIR

Every administrator is unique and most often it is difficult to get a substitute for an able and efficient administrator. Some of the Chairs are never filled; and the void they create leads to collapse of organizations, companies and even countries.

I did not know the importance of a Chair and the authority it holds, and the culture associated with it way into my high school days.

During my elementary school days, once the principal of our school had to attend a meeting and hence the authority was transferred to my teacher for a couple of days. He never sat on the principal's chair. The chair was unique that it was the only revolving chair in the entire School. I was a fourth-grade kid and I always wanted to sit on that revolving chair as I thought that would be fun. One day I went to my teacher to borrow a book. He was sitting on a chair opposite to the principal's chair. I asked my teacher, "May I use the revolving chair".

"No, you are not supposed to sit on someone's chair especially people of high authority," replied my teacher.

That year for vacation, I spend time at my uncle's house, who operated a business from the adjacent store. When he was busy doing some errands. I sat on his chair. Sometime later, my father came and saw me sitting on my uncle's chair.

He angrily stated, "Get out of the chair, you are not supposed to sit on the chair."

"He is just a kid, he can sit there," replied my uncle who was standing at the corner of the office.

"No, he is a responsible kid and should know what a chair signifies," replied my father.

Years later, as a high school student I spend the vacation time at my father's estate. The estate was one of the largest clove plantations in that part of the country that my father meticulously cultivated.

The second morning after my arrival my father said, "Get ready, we will take a walk and see what the employees are doing."

I sat on my father's chair and tied my shoes. My father was standing at the other end of the hall and stared at me. Well, that look had a ton of meaning. Since that time, I know the importance of a chair.

8. PLAY WITH WHAT YOU HAVE

One of the games we played as a child was cricket. My neighbor friend, who was younger than me, was a lousy player. Most often, in the middle of the game the ball would hit the "fourth stump" and he would run into the house crying, "Mama, my friend hit me with the ball."

Years passed. I didn't know that my friend was seeking an opportunity to get over me. One day, I was asked to pick him early from Sunday school. He said, "We are planning a soccer game for 30 minutes, are you willing to play."

"Yes,' I replied.

"I will select my team," stated my friend. He selected all the boys from higher grades who were there for the game. I was left with the smaller boys, grades 3-6. There was no chance that our team would win the game. I also did not want to lose the game to my younger friend. I would be hearing for my entire life that I lost to him.

Before the game I called all the team members and said, "Chances are that we may not win this game, NEITHER WILL WE LOSE".

The game was tough. The kids played really well.

I was the goalkeeper. Whenever the ball was near our goal post, the kids formed a wall in front of me. Fortunately, the opposing team did not have the skills of David Beckham, hence the ball did not fly above the human wall.

At the end of game, it was 0-0.

My friend was grumbling, "If not for the small kids forming a wall, we would have won the game."

In life, we may have limited resources when running different projects. Work hard with what you have.

9. THE EDITOR

In school, every class had to bring out their own class magazine every year. At the start of every academic year the students would contribute couple of rupees for the manuscript magazine. The editors selected by the students would write legibly the articles contributed by the students. The manuscripts would later be bound in a press and the magazine released by the principal at the school assembly.

I always longed to publish an article in the class magazine. Unfortunately, for many years my articles were never selected for publication in the class magazine.

On the last day of my seventh grade, my classmate Vijay gifted me a pocketbook. The cover of the book depicted a flowering tree branch.

During summer vacation, I copied the tree branch in a book and colored it. The picture turned to be good. Since I had nothing else to do, I painted more pictures in the book.

When the school opened after vacation, I showed the pictures to Vijay and other students sitting beside me. That week, the teacher talked about the class magazine and asked for suggestions for the editorial board of the magazine. When the nominee of "art editor" was raised, my bench mate Ciju, pointed at me, "He is a good artist, I would recommend him." I was selected as the art editor of the class magazine. Little did I know that the title would impact my career forever.

A couple of weeks later, the "treasurer" brought some papers for the magazine. The quality of the paper was so bad that it could not be used for the magazine. We lost money on the paper. We had now limited budget to complete the magazine.

I used to go to school and back home in the school bus. En route was a stationary store with a printing press by its side located at a junction. Since my father was at home only during the weekends, I had to do everything on my own. The school bus would pass by the store at the junction, would go around a nearby college, return to the junction and proceed to the south of the city. In those days, the city was not very populated, and the traffic was less. I checked my watch; it would take around 7 minutes for the school bus to go around the college and return to the junction.

I had an idea. The bus conductor was in good terms with me. I asked the bus conductor if he could drop me near the stationary store and pick me back within seven minutes on its way to the south side of the city. He agreed.

When the bus stopped at the junction, I rushed straight to the stationary store. I talked to the owner of the stationary store about the class magazine. The owner said, "We have a poster paper. It is large and cost around one rupee. One-fourth the size of the poster paper is enough for the magazine." He also gave me a sample. The business was done within 5 minutes.

The editorial board was pleased with the choice and price of the paper. The next day I dashed from the school bus and purchased 25 sheets of poster paper. The press cut it into 100 sheets. We worked hard on the magazine and within a couple of months completed the class magazine.

Once the magazine was completed, like previous occasions I dashed from the school bus and ran to the printing press. I negotiated with the press and got a good deal for binding the magazine. All the business was done under 5 minutes! The class magazine turned out to be one of the largest magazines in school and one of the best published that year. It was also cheaper than most class magazines of that year. I handed over the remaining money to the class teacher.

I learned not only how to edit magazines, but also the business of book making. Years later I became the author, editor and executive of several books and publications.

Where there is a will, there is a way. Never give up hope. You will achieve whatever you have dreamed.

10. HUMILITY

I learned photography in the middle school. One year after learning photography we went for vacation to our father's plantation.

My father had an aid, Mr. Raj, who was working at the plantation for many years. Raj was a movie buff, he watched movies whenever he went to town.

There was a garden in front of the house. On a clear day I asked my parents to sit for a photo-shoot. While taking the picture, Raj came behind me. He said, "Why don't you have the flowers in the foreground of your parents while taking the picture."

I took the picture as Raj had envisioned. The picture turned out to be one of the best pictures I had taken.

When my mother saw the pictures she was surprised I was good at photography. She said, "Good that you followed Raj's advice. You could have ignored him. Since you were humble, you got a good photograph. I am sure you will be proud of your achievement for many years."

Be humble. Do not ignore others voice.

11. POSTER

We decided to describe the continental drift on a poster during our school science exhibition. However, both of us had no idea to draw the continents on a poster. I had some experience drawing cartoons, my friend could not draw anything!

While we were pondering how to proceed, a classmate heard our discussion. He said, "My sister knows to draw, maybe she can help you out."

We were glad, we handed the blank poster sheet to our classmate.

A couple of days later, our classmate brought the completed poster. We were thoroughly disappointed seeing the poster. It was unfit to be displayed!

I said," Seeing the quality of this work, I think I can do a better job."

I went home and worked on the empty reverse side of the poster. The poster looked perfect and very professional. Until then I didn't know that I could draw the earth and its continents.

Everyone has hidden talents. Discover your hidden talents.

12. DISCOVER YOURSELF

It is said that failure begets success. Failure is an engine that could motivate a person for life. Students who do not perform well during school days often perform well later, in the University and beyond.

Life is a long road where failures define you. Failures teach you things that you had no intention to learn when life is in "normal mode". Often, managing your life gracefully is enough to get out of failure. Discipline is the first step to a successful life.

Each person is unique; talents are acquired by learning. Time is crucial for learning. Our head is like a fort. For an army to conquer the fort, they have to blast the fort repeatedly. Similar is our brain. Some people have photogenic memory; they can immediately comprehend a concept by reading a book, a single time. For others, they have to read the book multiple times to understand a concept. Sometimes, to understand a concept, some students have to read the topic written by multiple authors. People are different and some of us have to work harder than others to achieve success.

While in school Ashton was an average student. Ashton's days started at 5:30 AM; whether he completed his studies or not he went to bed at 10:00 PM. Ashton's grades were always a B+.

The eleventh and twelfth grades are crucial for any student. In the first exam of the eleventh grade Ashton scored low grades in a couple of subjects.

Ashton said to himself, "If I do not do well, I will never get into a good college."

Ashton pondered how he could improve his grades. The only way to improve his grades, was to work hard and work smart. He made up his mind not to go to bed until he finished learning whatever was taught in class. Everyday he woke up at 4:30 AM to study. Since Ashton was not a very bright student, he went to the library and read books written by different authors on the same subject. For learning math, physics and chemistry, he wrote whatever was taught 3-5 times, everyday.

The tests conducted a month later was easy for Ashton. His grades improved eventually. He graduated high school with good grades and pursued higher education at a good university.

In one of the University tests, Ashton was given only thirty days to prepare. Ashton asked his friend Philip to help him. Philip took him to the library and showed all the books that would be helpful for the test.

Ashton read one book each day to prepare for the test. The test was easy for Ashton. He was a topper in the test.

Every person is unique. You have to discover who you are. Every student comprehends things differently. Some students have to work harder than others.

13. PASSION

During my University days I used the University lodging facility. The food was provided in the dining hall. One of the requirements for staying at the University residence was that the students had the responsibility to run the mess facility. Every student who was selected at random, either alone or as a group would have to run the mess facility for a month. The students don't have to cook, there were cooks and assistants to take care of it. However, the students running the mess facility were responsible for buying the groceries every week.

At the end of my first year at the University I was selected to run the mess facility. Unfortunately, as it was the end of the year many students left for home. Hence, I did not have any partners to help me with the chores.

The first week I asked a friend, who was an athlete for help. He received several awards from the University in athletics and other games. I took him to the city for grocery shopping. It was not fun; we had to walk to different stores selling different produce. I had to negotiate with different businesses to get the best deals. Less than half-way into the ordeal I noticed my friend was very tired and panting. Seeing his face, I knew he had no interest in doing the work. Since the errand took plenty of time, I asked him to get back to the University; and he was happy to leave!

If you are not passionate, no matter how small the work, you get tired.

14. PENALTY

Millions of people go to bed on an empty stomach due to lack of food. More than thirty percent of food is wasted or rotten before it reaches the consumer. In addition, a good number of people waste their food.

One of the requirements staying at the University residence was that students would have to oversee the food distribution in the dining hall. Once I was selected for the job for a month. I had seen several students wasting food. Coming form an agriculture family I know how hard it is to produce food. The farmer has to fight microbes, insects, rodents, birds to get a good crop. In addition, in some years, weather also takes a toll on the food produced. I introduced a new rule: Anyone wasting food would be fined Re. 1 for the offense.

Some of the students protested. I did not blink. However, many students voluntarily entered the ledger book when they wasted food. The cooks were happy that the food was not wasted.

I hear one student lamenting, "It is not the amount of money that bothers me, but the term "fine."

At the end of the month, the dining fees was lower compared to the previous months.

Harsh rules deter bad behavior and ultimately help the society.

15. WANDERING EYES

Most of the campus of public universities and colleges of developing countries are not kept clean. During my final year of my post-graduate course, we had a new Vice Chancellor at the University.

I used to go the laboratory early morning for work. While walking to the laboratory, I used to see the Vice Chancellor of the University, Prof. K.G. Adiyodi and his wife, Rita Adiyodi walk around the campus. Any bits of paper or trash on the campus were removed. The campus was clean and tidy when he was in office. Ironically, his successors never bothered to take care of the campus.

Every person occupying a position has different intentions. Some people take up leadership position for the fame associated with it, either in the family or among peers. Whereas, some people take up the leadership position for making a genuine change. Change makes the world a better place to live.

16. COLLEGE FEES

The three year public college education in India was not expensive until the late 1990's. During that period it was damn cheap to study at the University College, Trivandrum, India. Looking at the exorbitant college fees of the present era I reflect on the "old days" of college education. Back then, the monthly fees was just Rs. 18.00; the public bus fare per month for students was just Rs. 3.50. Even a meal with coffee at the nearby Indian Coffee House would cost only Rs. 5.00. But there was a catch going to public colleges for studies in those days – strike! Yes, you never know when the teachers would go on strike in those days. Hence, we had to go for private tuition after class; and those were affordable too for every families.

University College offered everything for students. If you wished to study, you could study; if you wished to loaf around, there were plenty of activities in the surroundings. As most students were from middle class families, they attended every class; or they could not quit classes because others were attending the class ("peer pressure"). I had set my eyes on higher education; hence had to toil hard. Any free time was spent at the college library or the adjacent Kerala University Library, Public Library or reading text books in the empty language class room ("cattle shed"). Occasionally, some students came to discuss about movies while I sat in the last bench reading text books in the "cattle shed". Some of those students who came to discuss movies later turned to be artists in Indian movies.

Being a student of Botany, we had to work on herbarium. We had to submit the herbarium by the end of third year. During the final year I collected some seeds of "Chembakam" (*Magnolia champaca*) from the college botanical garden. Seeing me collecting the seeds some of my colleagues also followed me. Those seeds were planted in plastic bags. After a couple of weeks, there were plenty of saplings in our backyard. I asked my colleagues the status of their plants. They said none of them grew. Hence, I gave some saplings from my collection to my classmates.

Eventually, after several months of growth, those Chembakam saplings landed in our family home. Two of them grew to tall trees. However, there was only occasional flowering in those trees. As the tree grew very tall, my parents had the top of the trees cut to prevent lighting strike. Several decades passed, the trees started shedding plenty of leaves and it was difficult to keep the surroundings clean. My parents decided to dispose of those trees. They asked a lumberman the buying price of the Chembakam trees. "Rs. 6000."

Well, I calculated my three year college fees. The three year college, tuition, bus and study tour fees cost less than Rs. 5000. The two trees from the college garden paid off my college education fees!!

Gist of the story: Plant some trees when you are young, one day it will pay off your debt.

17. FAILING GRACEFULLY

The professor left the class after handing over the questions during a class test. The students glanced at the question paper. The questions were tough.

The students studied very hard before the exam. Upon seeing the questions, the class became nervous. One-by-one the students started discussing the answers as everyone was afraid of failure. The more successful you are, the higher the fear of failure.

Copying in exams is an art. Not everyone is good at it! I did not know the answer to half the questions. I did not dare ask anyone, nor showed my answers to others. Nobody also dared to ask me any answers.

After two hours, the professor returned to the class. She said, "I know the questions are tough, but if you have not copied or given out any answers to others, kindly state it at the end of the answer sheet. I will give you one mark for honesty."

I wrote the disclaimer at the end of the answer sheet.

When the results were announced everyone passed the test with good grades, except one. I failed, I was short of one mark. However, my disclaimer stating that I did not copy or provided any answers to others granted me one mark. I passed the test.

18. TWO EYES FOLLOW YOU

Whoever you are and whatever you do there are always a pair of eyes following you and your deeds.

When I was studying at the University I stayed at the University residence. There were around one hundred students living in the University residence. We did not have to wash our dishes, the cook and his assistant would take care of it. I do not waste any food after meals. The cook and his aide seldom showed up when we dined. One day the cook approached me after I had completed my dinner. He said, "There are around a hundred students here, but when everybody leaves, I know your dish and where you sat for dinner."

***

While at the University residence, I was one of the first to wake up every morning. Every morning when I wake up I used to get notes that the fellow students put under the door. I had to wake the students who don't trust their alarm. Those students went back to sleep after turning off their alarm; hence they would trust me waking them up.

When you work in your office or raise your children people follow you. Most often you do not know how your action and deeds motivate others.

38

19. DOING PH.D

Students ask me how difficult it is to work on a Ph.D. in science. Doing a Ph.D is a fusion of science and management.

How do you eat a pizza? You don't eat the whole pizza. You divide into 5-6 pieces and eat one by one.

When I started my Ph.D program, I divided the proposal into 5 topics. I worked on each topic, and submitted to journals. Most often, it came back for additional experiments. I worked on it quickly and published it.

The model was faster than expected. The whole proposal was completed in a period of 2.5 years. At that time, the average period of Ph.D work at the Institute was 6.0 years. My supervisor asked me to go slow, hence the final writing part was completed under a year.

Each published paper turned out be a chapter in the thesis. The final draft of the thesis went to the biggest critique of the Institute. I received it after a couple of weeks. I was surprised to see no comments on the thesis. I thought that he did not go through it. Later, one of his student told me that he tried hard to find any errors, but could not find any.

The reviewers also did not find any mistake or errors in the thesis (it was already corrected by many reviewers of journals). The defense reviewer stated that it was one of the finest thesis he had ever seen.

When you are working on a Ph.D., if you have a good supervisor, consider 50% of the work is over. If you have good colleagues, another 25% is over. You just have to work on the rest 25%.

20. THE TRASH OF SOMEONE IS A FORTUNE FOR ANOTHER

Everything has value. Most often we underestimate the value of materials.

During my research days a senior research professor of a nearby university working on her research thesis came to my laboratory for a visit.

I showed her our experiments and discussed the data that we generated in our laboratory. A couple of days earlier I had completed an Ouchterlony double diffusion experiment to determine the specificity of our antibody that we generated. I had also photographed the Petri dish that was used to run the Ouchterlony assay. I had left the Petri dish on the laboratory bench to see if there were any further changes with time. I planned to destroy the assay and re-use the Petri dish later. I showed the visitor the Petri dish and she was happy to see that such a small experiment provided useful and vital data. As I had an assignment in the city, I had to quickly leave the laboratory after talking to the visiting senior research professor. Before leaving, I also notified my supervisor. My supervisor also wanted to speak to the visitor on his other work done at the laboratory.

After a couple of hours, I came back to the laboratory. Alas, I could not see my Petri dish with the Ouchterlony assay! The visitor had taken it with her. Anyone who had access to the Ouchterlony assay could photograph it and use it in their thesis or paper!

I learned an important lesson that day. Anything you consider trash or a thing of less value is a fortune for others. You never know the intention of people coming for discussion at your workplace. Do not leave a visitor unattended or alone at your workplace or office.

Your official letterhead, business card, etc., should not be displayed on your table. Even a photograph with a stranger may be of value to the other person.

21. HEAD TO TOE

My college and university were in the tropics. The weather was humid. I wore a half sleeve shirt and sandals to the class. Some of my relatives used to complain my shabby dressing. During my research years I had an assistant, Mr. Santhosh who used to take care of the green house and vivarium. He never liked me working in the green house. He would always say, "It is my duty, you are not supposed to be here."

One summer, we had a seminar with external speakers from outside the Institute. I was one of the members assigned to welcome the guests. On that day I had to dress formal.

While arranging the brochure, Santhosh passed by. He looked me from head to toe and walked away.

The next day I was checking my plants at the green house. Santhosh came to me, "I think you should wear the formal dress everyday. As you are working in the laboratory you look more professional."

Everyone has the right to his/her opinion. People will speak their opinion directly if they are interested in you. It is your choice to act on the opinion.

22. THE POSTDOC

Many months into working as a postdoctoral fellow at the Dept. of Biochemistry, Indian Institute of Science (IISc), Bangalore, India, I had a visitor in our laboratory. He introduced himself as a Ph.D student at Prof. CJB's laboratory. He was with the professor for five years. However, his Ph.D was only half-way through. The professor had requested him to see me and get my guidance to complete his Ph.D.

My laboratory closed at 5:00 PM; since I had nothing else to do I would be at the library reading science, management and technology books and journals.

I talked with Mr. Subash about his project, his goals, and aspirations. He had a good research project; however, he was not focused.

Frankly, IISc was not an Institute I enjoyed working. The environment was very boring with no cooperation between the students. Most of them were tensed and hardly smiled. I doubt whether the projects done at IISc had any relevance to India; however, they were fit to be published in high impact journals and they remained there forever!

I had the gut feeling that I would not be at IISc for very long. Hence, I chalked out a plan with

Mr. Subash to do some "easy experiments" that could quickly test his scientific hypotheses. We started our work sometime in June 2001. I worked with him late into night. Everyday around 12:00 AM I would take him to the cafeteria and get him snacks and hot coffee so as to re-charge ourselves. Often, we would work until 2:00 AM.

Once Mr. Subash had a minor accident in the laboratory and he could not use his left hand. I told him, "You have one hand, and I have two. That is enough for this work." Luckily, all our experiments had picture-perfect results. By September, we finished all the experiments and also completed the Ph.D dissertation. In early October I helped him write his curriculum vitae (CV) and also crafted a good cover letter. Exactly twenty-four hours after sending his CV, he got a reply from the University of Pennsylvania, Philadelphia informing him that they were willing to employ him as a postdoctoral fellow. He took up that job. October 31, 2001, I took Mr. Subash to the airport and bid farewell. Thirteen days later I am at New York City, where I started working for my second postdoctoral research.

Many years later the student became a CSO of a biopharma company.

There is nothing satisfying as working with someone to achieve his/her dreams.

23. THE CROW

The young man moved to a new town for his first job. He was from a wealthy family; however, his families business nose-dived a couple of years before his first job. He struggled during his education due to lack of resources. However, he worked hard and received his first job within months of completing his education. He rented an unfurnished home near his office. Due to lack of money, he furnished his house slowly, from his savings every month.

The young man lamented his misfortune and bad luck. One day while he was waiting for a bus, he noticed a crow building a nest on a nearby tree. The crow would collect twigs and leaves one-by-one and construct the nest. The young man also thought what would happen once the hatching season is over. Once the chicks fly away, the parents also move out and the crow nest is destroyed by the elements. The next generation would have to build a new nest. The crow at the bus stop taught him an important lesson.

The young man worked hard and many years later was the owner of an apartment complex renting apartments to families.

In life you cannot rely on the fortunes of your parents or siblings. Sometimes you must start everything from scratch, and it is worth the effort.

24. SAVING MONEY

I met a classmate after a long time. During our conversation on science, we talked about some scientific protocols and papers.

This was before the digital era. Since I had a large collection of journals, I said to her, "I will send you the copy of the papers that may be helpful to you along with the receipt. Kindly make sure you reimburse my money. You will be reimbursed when you submit the receipt at your office."

The library at our Institute was not very friendly. We were not supposed to copy anything directly. There was an officer who took care of copying journals. We had to literally beg to copy anything.

After having the copy of the papers, I posted the materials along with the receipt to my former classmate.

Several months passed, I did not receive any money. Once I went to the University for a meeting and I met my former classmate at her laboratory. During our conversation I asked about the papers and the receipt. "Oh, I received it."

When I asked about the promise of reimbursing the money, she smiled at me.

Many months passed; I received a wedding invitation from my classmate. I could not attend the wedding as I had an important meeting on that day.

After some months, I had a chance to see my classmate. She said, "I send you a wedding invitation, you did not attend my wedding."

I looked up into her eyes and said, "You were supposed to give me Rs. 100 for the papers I sent you, which you never did. If I came to your wedding, it would have cost me Rs. 500. Deducing Rs. 100, I saved Rs. 400 by not attending your wedding."

You cannot make people happy all the time. Don't let others treat you like a doormat.

25. JUICE

One evening, after a tedious work in the laboratory I was thinking of having a juice. I had more work to do. After work, I also had to walk 30 minutes to reach home. I took the juice in my hand......."Maybe I will have it later, before going home."

Our laboratory was a large hall with multiple investigators. My colleague, Ivanka was working with another professor. The professor was not very social with her students. She extracted her students, everyday, like people handling the last drops of a tube of tooth paste. However good the student performed, at the end of the day the professor would find fault in the student's work.

On the fateful day, Ivanka was having a hard time with her professor. Ivanka had to present a poster at the Annual Academy Day the following day; and she had no experience presenting a poster in her life. At 10:00 PM, before the professor left, she gave Ivanka cell culture work that had to be done immediately. In addition, the professor commented to her that her work was lousy. She also never bothered to discuss the poster before leaving.

The negative comments had a toll on Ivanka. She broke down. She was in tears while working on the cell culture. My work was almost over by that time. Everyone had left the laboratory.

I felt sorry for Ivanka. I gave her the fruit juice that I planned to have before going home. Luckily, she calmed down after having the juice. While having the juice I said, "We will have the trial of the poster presentation after your work."

"Thank you."

She was sobbing during her work after my conversation with her. Sometime later, her husband Ashton called her on the laboratory phone. I picked up the phone. I knew that if I let Ivanka talk, she will break down. Ashton used to work there before, and he knew the work culture of the laboratory.

"What is Ivanka doing? It is 11:00 PM."

I bluffed in a low voice, "The professor is here, she is working with Ivanka. Your wife is working on some cell culture."

If I had given the phone to Ivanka, the tear gates would open. Hence, I attended the phone.

After 40 minutes, the phone rang again.

I again picked up the phone. I said in a bolder voice, "The professor just left. Ivanka is working. She just conveyed to me that she will finish before 1:00 AM."

I looked at Ivanka. She was smiling.

"Okay, we will start working on the poster once you complete your cell culture."

By 12:00 AM Ivanka completed her cell culture. Ivanka did her presentation, and I gave suggestions to improve.

Ten hours later Ivanka presented her poster at the Academy. That evening she came back to the laboratory to see me.

Ivanka had a smile from ear to ear. "I won the best poster award. Thank you for your generosity and training."

The flowing day during lunch she took me to the break room. There was a sumptuous display of different dishes waiting for me.

If you see your colleagues in a hopeless situation, stand beside them. In such situations you will have to work patiently to put a smile on your colleagues. You have to advice like a friend, or a family member to lighten the gloomy day.

26. THE SHOE

I am particular how a student dress up when they show up at the laboratory.

One of the world's famous hospital is Mayo Clinic. When a staff comes in, the authorities check how they are dressed, from head to toe. If the shoelace is soiled, they ask to change it!

I expect the students to be in full sleeves, regular pants (not jeans). The women should have their hair tied up when they are in the laboratory. The men should have their face fully shaved. I explicitly state these. I don't have any feelings what they think of me. I also ask them not to use their cell phone in the laboratory. One time I asked a student to sign that she will not use the cellphone in the lab (as she was abusing her phone). (If not signing, "leave").

One day a student came to the laboratory in a broken shoe. I asked, "What happened to your shoe?"

"Broken, while travelling in the subway."

The next day, he again showed up in the broken shoe. This time he wrapped with a tape!!

"What, you don't have money to buy a shoe?"

"I used up the money given by my parents. I have to wait another month to get the next installment from my parents."

I said, "Follow me".

"Where?"

I walked to the parking area and opened the car door. "Get in."

"Where are we going?"

"Wear your seat belt."

I took him to the nearest department store and headed straight to the shoe section. "Select whatever you like."

He said, "These are expensive."

"Don't care about the money, take what you like. Discard your old shoe right here."

"Thank you."

Two days later he knocked on my door with some money. He was extending his hand with the money.

I said to him, "Go to work man. Keep the money with you."

Today he is an engineer at a large company.

There are sacrifices at your end if you wish to run an organization the way you want.

27. CUTTING CORNERS

One winter, James was invited to a party in the city. On the way it was heavily snowing. When he reached the destination, the street was completely parked with cars; there was no parking spot. Luckily, James found a snow piled area. As the street parking was too tight, he hit the snow pile and parked his vehicle with the front end inside the snow pile. James was happy that he found a parking spot.

Once he entered the house, the snowfall increased, and it turned to sleet at night. The host asked James to stay at his house as it was dangerous to drive.

The next day, James bid farewell to the host and went to his vehicle. James reversed his vehicle. R-R-I-I-P-P....he heard a sound. James came out of his vehicle and saw that his vehicle's bumper was ripped off. Apparently, the snow solidified overnight and destroyed the bumper.

Sometimes things get messed up when you try to cut corners.

28. FEEDBACK

To improve yourself, you receive feedbacks from your parents, teachers, friends or supervisors. If the feedback is genuine you should take the message seriously and work on it. However, not everyone gives the correct feedback and not everyone take the feedback seriously.

Companies also receive feedback from clients or reports from the press. Several companies have improved their products based on the feedback. Those companies not only improved their products but also increased the market share. Likewise, companies that don't heed to feedback die a natural death.

While working at a laboratory in New York City, we used to buy diagnostic reagents from a German company. The company claimed one hundred reactions could be performed by its diagnostic kit. Unfortunately, we could only get 90 reactions. I talked about this problem to the sales representative.

A couple of weeks later, the sales representative came to the laboratory with a woman in tow. The sales representative came and introduced the lady.

"This is the Product Manager of our company. She came this morning from Germany. Kindly state your concerns regarding the diagnostic kit to the Manager."

I was surprised that they took my feedback seriously. Eventually we figured out the reason why the numbers were different than the number claimed by the company.

Take feedback seriously.

29. THE CRITIQUE

Christopher, my colleague at the Institute was completing his Ph.D. A day before his final presentation Christopher invited a couple of us for the mock presentation.

The mock presentation turned out to be a disaster. We asked several questions based on his work. Christopher could not stand the heat. He was completely stressed out. He could not take the questions anymore. He angrily blurted, "GET OUT."

We said, "We are doing our duty."

We remained in the hall until the end of the mock presentation. However, Christopher took our questions seriously. That night Christopher worked on the questions raised by us.

The next day, during the final presentation the professors asked Christopher the same questions that we raised the previous day. Since Christopher was prepared, he answered all the questions clearly.

When the professors and examiners left the hall after the presentation, Christopher came to us and thanked profusely, "I owe you."

"When is the treat?"

"Tomorrow."

Better get "killed/hammered" during the mock presentation than during the final presentation.

30. THE NEXT GENERATION

Everyone was awestruck at the beautiful tree in front of our house. I was also proud of the tree that changed color every season. The canopy was umbrella shaped. The vibrant color of the tree's foliage contrasted with the green lawn.

The majestic tree shed large number of seeds in the fall season. However, I showed no mercy to the saplings. The lawn mower got rid of all the saplings while mowing the lawn.

Then one day, a lightning struck. The tree fell.

Unfortunately, there was not a single sapling around to be planted as a replacement for the majestic tree.

Replace this scenario with organizations and companies. Often, most organizations do not cultivate the next leaders. When a leader of an organization leaves, it is difficult to find a replacement as there are no internal candidates with the knowledge, passion, or acumen. Hence, the organization is forced to look for a new leader from outside.

31. TIME

It was a rainy day; the single lane road was slippery. We were travelling slowly. There were not many vehicles on the road. However, the lone car in front of us was extremely slow.

My son, sitting behind, calmly said, "Dad, why don't we overtake the car."

I said, "It is against rules to overtake. Moreover, the vehicle may not stay always in front of us. He may turn to a side road any moment."

Just as I stated, after a couple of minutes, the driver ahead of us diverted to a side road.

I was the only one driving on the empty road. I drove on the empty road at my pace!

Sometimes in life we have someone ahead of us that is a stumbling block. It is just a matter of time. After some time, they move out of your life and you will be leading. Be patient until then.

32. CLOSED DOOR

In the lobby of a building when the elevator door opened, I saw a person still standing in front of a closed door. She failed to notice the open door. I notified her about the open door. When the person stepped in, I said, "This is life. Often we stand in front of the closed door without noticing the open door."

'True."

When Turks captured Constantinople, the Western European kingdoms lost access to the Malabar Coast, India to trade spices. Eventually they found a way to reach India. In addition, they discovered several continents that were unheard before.

When a small door closes, a large door opens.

33. EVERYBODY HAS A CHANCE

Once I took my colleague to the upper deck of the Empire State Building, New York to see the beautiful New York City skyline and beyond. I had been to the Empire State Building several times and knew the behavior of the visitors.

It was a beautiful day, and the upper deck of the Empire State Building was crowded. My colleague wished to take some pictures of the city. However, nobody moved from their position.

I said, "It is windy over here. Nobody is going to stay by the parapet forever."

Just as I stated, people moved away from the parapet after 5-10 minutes. We photographed the city skyline for more than an hour.

In life, everybody has a chance to fulfill his/her wishes.

34. THE FENCE

The deer are a menace around our suburban house. In the previous year the children cultivated some vegetables; however, once the vegetables were almost mature and ready to be harvested, the deer had a feast on a dark cloudy night.

The only way to cultivate anything around our house was to put a fence around a plot of land. Our contractor neighbor Santo helped us with the garden improvement project.

Once the fence went up, the children planted several types of vegetables, including summer squash. The summer squash is a creeper and an occasional climber, and it does what it is supposed to do, climb the fence! The climber put out flowers inside the fence as well as outside the fence. Some of the branches were also seen outside the fence. Within weeks we could see summer squash everywhere. However, the summer squash outside the fence was larger and heavier than the ones inside the fence. It seemed that those summer squash that enjoyed freedom outside were happier and more successful!

The same is true for societies. Those societies that enjoy limited freedom and are confined with restrictions are not happy. Such societies are not very creative; in fact, they are prevented from being creative and eventually the country has stunted growth. However, those societies that enjoy unlimited freedom are more creative, work harder and eventually the country gets richer.

35. THE APPLE TREE

There was a row of apple trees by the side of a factory. It was planted by one of the founders of the factory. The founder's children used to play and have fun at the orchard. The apple trees were healthy and flowered every spring. It did not require any pesticide or fertilizers. The fruits were sweet and tasty, and the workers in the factory were offered the apples by the company just before the fall season.

Many years passed and a new manager was put in charge of the factory. He did not like the apple trees. He cut off the trees without consulting the factory owners.

The new manager planted new hybrid apples. However, the new apple trees required constant care. They required plenty of fertilizers, pesticides and water. The apple trees did not produce enough fruit as anticipated by the manager. Eventually, the manager lost interest in the new apple trees.

Once the owner visited the factory and saw the apple trees and the cost to maintain it. He was planning to build new offices for the factory. He asked the contractor to cut down the unproductive apple trees and build new offices in its place.

Sometimes you see managers or CEO's harassing very productive workers for various insignificant reasons. Once the toxic situation reaches the tipping point these productive workers leave. New workers with higher salaries are recruited in place of the ones productive workers who had left the company. Often, these new workers may not be productive as anticipated.

36. CHAIR-CAR CEO

When I started working at an Institute, I wished to see the Director of the Institute. My laboratory was at the far end of the building, whereas the Director's office was near the main entrance. I never saw the Director for the first four months. Apparently, he always came to the office in the Institute's chauffeur driven car. After stepping out of the car he headed straight to his office. In the evening, once the work was over for the day, the Director headed back to his car.

One day, after four months of work at the Institute; someone came to talk to my supervisor while discussing my data. After he left, I asked my supervisor who was the person. He replied, "It is the Director of this Institute."

Several years later, the Director retired. A new Director was assigned.

The new Director was entirely different compared to the former; he had a different work culture. He walked on the corridor every morning and afternoon. He had an idea what was happening at the Institute. The empty spaces around the Institute were transformed into mini gardens. He motivated the people of the Institute and the productivity increased.

Gist of the story: If you are a CEO or a Director of an organization, make sure you walk around the organization at least once a day. Your presence motivate and encourages the employees.

37. CHAUFFEUR

This was one of the folklores while working in my first organization. The Director had to attend a meeting in a far-away city. He was taken to the city in the chauffeur driven car of the organization. It was late evening, the chauffeur was tired after driving for several hours, and wished to have a cup of coffee. He stopped the car in front of a café. While stepping out of the car he looked back and found the Director to be asleep. He did not want to disturb his boss; hence, he went to the coffee shop to have a cup of coffee. Returning, the chauffeur failed to notice the back seat of his car. After driving many miles, the chauffeur turned back to see if his boss was still asleep.

"WHAT! The boss is missing." Seat belts were not popular during that time. The chauffeur had scary thoughts, "Did the boss fall off from the car while driving?"

He turned around and headed to the coffee shop. Luckily, he did not see anyone lying on the road. When he reached the coffee shop, he saw the Director having a cup of coffee.

Even in familiar situations look around.

38. HOW TO CATCH FISH WITHOUT WETTING YOUR HANDS

Living in Galveston, Texas was a big contrast compared to our life in New York City. Galveston is a large sandy island. For fun activities, there were limited options: either spend time on the beach or go fishing or crabbing. The piers on the island jutting into the Gulf of Mexico were a popular area for fishing and crabbing. My wife would accompany me while fishing or crabbing. Catching crabs were relatively easy. However, fishing was time consuming. My wife was always lucky that whenever she put in the reel, she caught fish. I would always say that they were "boys."

During weekends the piers were crowded. Some people came to fish on the fishing pier as a hobby. Once they caught fish, they would show everyone and ask if someone wanted it. If people were not interested, they would return the catch into the sea.

Since I was not so lucky in catching fish, I would wave my hand if a lucky angler waved his fish. Seeing my interest in the fish, several anglers would wave at me when they caught fish. Within an hour our bucket would be full. Once full I would say, "We have enough fish, we will go home."

On the way home my wife would say, "One day you should write a book on how to catch fish without wetting your hands."

39. TRAFFIC LIGHT LESSONS

The speed of your vehicle is directly proportional to the traffic light signal on the road.

* * *

The green light signal transition to yellow before turning to red. The same is true in life. When you are a leader or successful in a field, sometimes the yellow light turns on. Those yellow light incidences need immediate attention. If you do not take care or do not pay attention, you will "land in soup" after some time. Incidences that need attention can vary and may include lack of innovation of your products, high cost of products, behavioral like abuse of alcohol, wrong friendship or not taking care of your health.

* * *

If you are an optimist when you see the red light you say, "I am early, hence, I have to wait some time."

If you are a pessimist, once you see the red light you will be cursing. Your thoughts will be, "I should have been at least ten seconds early, now I have to wait for thirty seconds."

* * *

Occasionally when you are the first come to a stop in front of a red signal, you think you will be the first to race ahead. However, often you must have seen a fellow traveler out of nowhere zooming past you when the lights turn green.

Same is true in business. You never know when a competitor shows up when you think you are a leader of the domain.

40. THE NAPKIN

Everything has a purpose in life. As a human it is our responsibility to figure out our purpose in life. Even a simple napkin has a purpose in life. Its purpose is to clean up a mess. I am sure every napkin does its job before landing in the garbage can.

Some of the napkins turned out to be more successful than it was meant to be. Looking at the history of companies, several of them who were successful later, were conceived on a piece of napkin. Several successful ideas were born on a piece of napkin in the laboratories.

41. THE BIOSIMULATOR

One of the initial projects assigned to me at the Institute was to develop an *in vivo* diagnostic based on indoleamine 2, 3-dioxygenase (IDO-1) for cancer studies. I developed a new hybridoma cell line for the project to make monoclonal antibodies. The hybridomas are non-adherent cells. They float in the medium. One day I saw a group of hybridoma cells adhering to a small scratch on a Petri dish. I asked a question: Is it possible to convert non-adherent cells to adherent cells?

I engraved Petri dishes that was never modified since its invention; the hybridoma cells were cultured in these modified dishes. The cells adhered to the engraving. It also showed polarity. At least in the initial days, the hybridoma had affinity to one side of the engrave, not to the opposite side. The engraved dish was later named the Biosimulator.

The Biosimulator was also used in the microbiome projects. It is known that most bacteria are non-culturable. The Biosimulator was used to culture bacteria from different environments. The Biosimulator could induce proliferation of some of the bacteria that could not be cultured by conventional methods.

The IDO-1 mAb developed was later licensed to a company.

Research is like a Russian doll. You never know the surprises hiding in your main project. Most people ignore new discoveries or findings by labelling them as "artifact". In fact, most of my significant findings were "hidden gems" in projects.

Think differently. Ask new questions. Be curious and creative. Publish/patent.

42. OPPORTUNITY

In 2015, the series editor of the Methods in Molecular Biology (MiMB), the prestigious book series of Springer-Nature approached me if I could contribute a book on Vaccine Design. I did not have any experience writing a book; however, I had experience writing dissertations and journal papers. Anyway, I stated I was interested in publishing a book.

In 2015, MiMB had 1400 books published since 1980 by famous scientists on different topics on science. On an average the books are around 300 pages, authored by 2-3 editors. The series editor had given limited freedom and one year to complete the book project. He also requested to get the consent form from each contributor once the chapter was received.

Since I knew the personality of professors and scientists I took a different approach (you will hear excuses after 6 months on why they are not contributing).

I am a regular reader of Harvard Business Review (HBR). Many years back I read an article on the importance of a good cover letter in eliciting collaboration. I drafted a good cover letter; I also requested the authors to send the consent form 24 hours after acceptance of invitation.

I requested my old colleague professors to contribute. Some of them questioned, "Do you have any experience publishing books?"

"No."

I never received any chapters from them. Apparently, people ask for experience for every job, except marriage.

Within a record time of 8 months I received 103 chapters (2500 pages). When I finally submitted the manuscript to the publisher, he said; "WHAT, IMPOSSIBLE. We are not going to publish this as a single book. Cut into two."

The book was published as a two volume book. The books Vaccine Design: Methods and Protocols, Vol. 1. Vaccines for Human Diseases and Vol. 2. Vaccines for Veterinary Diseases was one of the most read books published in the MiMB series. In five years, they had a combined download of 500,000.

43. THE MANAGER

Seven months after publishing the Vaccine Design books in 2016, I received a chapter on adjuvants from a professor. The chapter was well written. The professor never send me the consent form and I had no idea that he would submit the chapter.

Anyone would have said, "Sorry, you are late, we published the book."

A good manager provides hope in a hopeless situation.

I said, "We already published the book, but hold on to it. I will be in touch with you in 24 hours."

I touched base with my contacts at the publishing house. "Do you know anyone in the world working on a book on Vaccine Adjuvants?"

A couple of hours later, I received a reply that an author at Washington State will be submitting a book on the topic in one week. He also forwarded his details.

I quickly contacted the author and got a positive reply. I later contacted the professor and his chapter eventually made into the book.

Every manager will face challenges. Ultimately you are responsible for putting a smile on the face of your people.

44. EASTERN BLOTTING

The blotting techniques are the work horses in biomedical laboratories. Blotting techniques are used in all areas of life sciences, including drug development. In the mid 1970's Edwin Southern developed the Southern blotting technique to detect DNA.

Later, George Stark and his colleagues at Stanford University developed the northern blotting technique (a play on the name Southern) to detect RNA. The laboratories of Neal Burnette (Fred Hutchinson Cancer Center, Seattle), George Stark (Stanford University) and Harry Towbin (Friedrich Miescher-Institute, Switzerland) independently developed the western blotting technique to detect proteins.

Scientists thought that there will never be an eastern blotting technique as the then existing blotting techniques could detect the fundamental molecules DNA, RNA and protein, and no further molecules were there to be detected.

In the early 2000's, I worked on T cell lipid rafts while working at the Mount Sinai School of Medicine, New York. I used cholera Toxin B to detect lipid moieties by the ELISA technique. After my post-doctoral days working in Immunology and Neuroscience, I moved to the University of Texas Medical Branch, at the island of Galveston in the Gulf of Mexico, off the coast of Texas.

My job was to develop a vaccine for ehrlichiosis. Ehrlichiosis is a disease caused by different species of the intracellular bacterial pathogen *Ehrlichia*.

First, I had to determine the major antigens of *Ehrlichia*. In the lab, we used two strains of *Ehrlichia* - *E. muris*, the non-virulent strain and IOE, the highly virulent strain. Both the strains had the same protein profile. This made me think, "What about protein modifications?"

There are around 30 post-translational protein modifications. I used the substrate cholera Toxin B to detect the lipid moieties; the non-virulent strain had high lipid modification on its antigenic proteins. Probing with substrate concanavalin A could determine the glycoproteins in the antigenic proteins. Further, I used a probe to detect phospho moieties.

I coined the term eastern blotting for the detection of post-translational protein modifications.

The term eastern blotting has since become popular and is now taught globally. In science, branding is important. Make sure you coin terms for a new phenomenon or technique that you discover.

45. THE KEYBOARD

One of the "dream" of my sister was to play a keyboard. With the help of a friend, she bought a Casio keyboard from the Middle East as keyboards were not very popular in India at that time. A tutor was assigned to teach the keyboard. Years passed, my sister graduated from college, married and moved to a neighboring city. Family life and the duties associated with it lost my sister's interest in playing the keyboard. The keyboard remained idle in the corner of a bedroom for many years.

One day a pastor came from a distant town to see my father, while en route to visit a rich family engaged in philanthropic activities. The pastor was running a small Church that also had retreat services. After the pastor left, my mother told father, "The keyboard is lying unattended for many years; maybe the pastor could use the keyboard. We should have donated it to the pastor."

After several hours the pastor came back to say that he is leaving for his town. He stated that he was unlucky that day as he could not meet the philanthropy family as they were away.

My father enquired to the pastor, "May I know if you are interested in a keyboard that was used by my daughter."

The pastor's eye brightened with joy, "I came to this town to visit the philanthropy family for fund raising purposes so that we could buy a keyboard for our small Church. I was really sad that I could not meet him today as he had to leave urgently for some business." "The good Lord works in mysterious ways." I am really interested in the keyboard and I could take it with me."

When the pastor left my mother called my sister and said that she "gifted" the keyboard to a small Church. My sister was really upset. "I had plans for my children. I wanted to teach them keyboard in a couple of years."

When I called my mother later that week, she told what happened to the keyboard. The following year I brought a Yamaha keyboard from New York and gifted it to my sister and her children. I said to my nephews, "When I come back next time, I would like to see that you play the keyboard really well; I also wish to hear at least five new musical scores created by each one of you."

Returning back to New York, I often inquired how my nephews were doing. Though the children were initially interested in music, with time they quit music. My mother was sad that her grandchildren quit music. The keyboard was left in a corner of a room unattended for a decade.

One day as I was readying to pack my bag to travel to India, my sister called me and said, "My children are not using the keyboard, better take it back and teach your children."

I did not want to lug the keyboard back to the US; hence, I asked my brother whether he wished to have the keyboard to teach his kids. "No, they have plenty of extracurricular activities. I don't think they have any time for a keyboard practice," replied my brother.

After a decade of "rest" the keyboard traveled back to the United States. My first-grade twins were taught to play the keyboard in October. They played the keyboard early morning and also after coming from school. The keyboard tutor encouraged the twins to play a small Christmas music on the first week of December. They repeated the same music for the Carol on Christmas Eve at our Parish Church. Six months after the Carol, the kids competed in a keyboard contest and won a prize! By the end of the summer the kids composed their own short musical scores; five of them, each.

46. FOOD POISON

One of the perks you enjoy working in biomedical laboratories is the different foods and treats provided by colleagues. In addition, if you have a sweet tooth, the colleagues will encourage to try their latest dishes.

Once I went to the physician's office for the regular check-up. The physician asked me to test the blood. A couple of weeks later he called me to his office.

"Your blood sugar level is in the borderline. Control your blood sugar. Rest are fine."

When I went back to my work, the exquisite food provided by my colleagues were staring at me. For me, from that moment, it was food poison.

47. THE LAST MINUTE

For some people the last minute of their sleep time is the best. Often times, you hope you had one more minute to stay in bed.

The quickest time of your examination may have been the last minute. Sometimes you wish you had an additional minute to complete your exam.

Wish you had left your home/office a minute earlier, to reach the destination on time.

Sometimes you wish you had that additional time on the project before submitting to your client.

48. REJECTION

What pattern do you see when you stir sugar while preparing lemonade? The moment you take away the spoon, the sugar forms a disc like structure at the bottom of the glass.

Many years back, I used potassium sulfate for protein purification. The potassium sulfate does not easily dissolve in water. However, heating potassium sulfate in water speeds up the dissolving process. After several minutes of stirring the hot water, potassium sulfate formed a spiral structure when settled at the bottom of the beaker. I used several other chemicals to see if it forms similar structure - none. I immediately understood that was a new phenomenon.

As I am not a chemist, I contacted researchers all over the world if they could explain why spiral structures are formed. Nobody had an explanation. One professor said. "Give me 3 years and X amount of money, I will find it out."

After my initial studies, I wrote about the new discovery and submitted the paper to a journal. They rejected as I failed to describe or even speculate a mechanism of spiral formation. I submitted to another journal….rejected. I improved the paper after each rejection. Every time the journal declined, some editors and reviewers speculated on the mechanism. After being rejected by 29 journals; yes, you heard it right 29 journals, I had some idea what causes the spiral structure (based on the feedback received). Finally, the Russian Journal of Physical Chemistry B accepted the paper for publication- five years after my first observation.

Never give up. Chase your dreams.

49. BIG HAT, NO CATTLE

There is a saying in Texas: Big hat, no cattle. It refers to those cowboys that have few cattle but put on a large hat to show-off. It also refers to someone who is all talk with no action, power, or substance behind his/her words.

Time and again I have seen students who are toppers in their class, resting on their laurels, doing nothing later in their life. Whereas, the back benchers who are not so talented, take off. They work hard and learn new skills and eventually motivate, lead, or influence the society.

In the Aesop's story of the hare and the tortoise, the hare sleeps thinking that he could beat the tortoise easily based on his skills, while the tortoise walk continuously, never giving up.

Education is a never-ending process. Whatever is taught in school is redundant in ten years. Most people throw their books in the river (stop reading) after their final exams. Whatever one learns in school or university is just a skeleton of knowledge. You have to add new knowledge everyday. Keep reading and also add to the knowledge based on your work and life experience.

You are like an airplane. You have to fly once your education is completed. A plane that does not fly is just a lame duck sitting idle. Most people put a period after completing their terminal education. In fact, it should be a comma.

Life did not stop with dinosaurs. It evolved. The world is evolving continuously. While travelling in an airplane, when we look out, we think the airplane is moving slowly. Most often we are flying close to one mach and reach the destination within a couple of hours. Life is like travelling on an airplane. Life moves faster than we think.

50. PURPOSE

Christopher Wren, a seventeenth-century English architect walked one day unrecognized among the men who were at work building the St. Paul's cathedral in London, which he had designed.

"What are you doing?" he inquired to one of the workmen. The man replied, "I am cutting a piece of stone." As Wren went on he asked the same question to another man, and the man replied, "I am earning five shillings two pence a day." To a third man he addressed the same question, and the man answered, "I am helping Sir Christopher Wren build a beautiful cathedral."

That man had a vision. He could see beyond the cutting of the stone, beyond the earning of his daily wage, to the creation of a house of prayer: the building of a great cathedral.

Centuries later President John F. Kennedy was visiting NASA headquarters for the first time in 1961. While touring the facility, he introduced himself to a janitor who was mopping the floor and asked him what he did at NASA. "I am helping put a man on the moon!" said the Janitor. The Janitor had a vision.

What is your purpose in life?

51. THE LAST ORDER

The "last order" by the parents in our family is the day we leave the house for our first job. My assignment was to use part of my salary, even if it was a meagre amount, for the betterment of society. (My father's "order" received from his parents while leaving the house was to take care of his employees… which he did extremely well to the end of his career).

I used part of my stipend (Rs. 250) to set up the Abraham Thomas Foundation. Over the years ATF used the limited resources for education, healthcare, helping small business, providing food during economic hardship, and biomedical research.

Non-profit organizations may be small, but their impact is big. You do not have to touch thousands of people, but lending a helping hand to just one person can make a big difference.

52. WRITING A CURRICULUM VITAE (CV)

A curriculum vitae (CV) is not a resume. A CV can be any number of pages; whereas a resume is just 2-3 pages. I have seen a 500 page CV.

You cannot judge a person from a resume. However, a CV shows all your accomplishments. You need to prepare a CV starting high school. If you are writing a CV early in life, it shows the gaps in your skills that you could improve or master. Delaying in writing a CV is costlier to you.

While writing CV, most people forget critical details...like scholarships received, presentations made, publications, working with non-profit organizations, leadership skills, technical skills, awards and honors, significant findings, patents, tutoring, etc.

Leadership skills include editorial roles, membership in committees, founder of companies, etc.

Volunteering includes working in nature reserves, working at old-age homes, food kitchen, or other community work.

If you are in management, show the figures (revenue earned and your contribution every year).

Show all your accomplishments in the job. If there is a ranking, state it. If you made an improvement in the organization show it.

If teaching, state how many students you trained, where they are, famous students...

If you received scholarship from grade 1-12; show it. It shows that you are consistent.

Technical skill also includes working with MS Office, Adobe Photoshop, statistical software, etc.

If you are a student fresh out of college, you could write all the laboratory skills, software, programming, hardware or machinery skills you mastered. Employers may be looking out for those skills.

In a CV, DO NOT write hobbies and sports (including karate, rifle shooting). It does not help your cause.

DO NOT pad your CV (bluff). People will pick on every statement written on a CV. You will be "in soup" if they think your CV looks fishy.

DO NOT state your religion, gender, name of parents, and date of birth. They are not relevant.

The last section is references. The references should be people you know (colleagues, friends, etc.). Ask the referees whether they would like to be your reference. Do not guess. (Someone who always smile at you does not mean he/she like you!!).

I have seen CV full of errors and spelling mistakes. Proofread your CV before submission.

Next time someone ask your resume, send your CV. It makes a huge difference.

A good CV could land you a scholarship (if pursuing higher education) or a good position in a great company.

53. COLORS

People are different. Even the siblings of a family have different character and personalities. Remember, in a classroom or office, people come from different environments.

I had a colleague, Ms. Laura who was emotional. One day Ms. Laura was in a sad mood, because someone said something that hurt her feelings.

I questioned her, "What color is the sky?"

"Blue."

What color is the grass over there?"

"Green."

What color is the flower on that tree?"

"Yellow."

What color is the building?"

"Red."

"Imagine if all these have the same color."

"Boring."

"The same is true with individuals. Every individual is unique. Imagine every individual having the same personality and character. The world would be boring."

54. BACK SEAT DRIVING

Whenever you take up a work, you might face hurdles. Learn to navigate the hurdles in your path.

At the university, I oversaw copying the textbooks for the class. I made sure that every student gets a copy of the study material within 16 hours after the class.

During the start of the genetics class, we did not have access to the textbook. The only copy of the book was with the professor. After the class, I asked the professor, "May I have the genetics textbook, I will return after copying."

"No."

I always hate hearing NO as an answer to a request. At that time, I was a dark, skinny, student. I came back to my class and approached the handsome student in our class. "Could you kindly borrow the genetics textbook from the professor for copying."

I did not tell him what happened earlier. After a few minutes he came back with the genetics textbook.

He handed the genetics textbook to me.

"Good job."

Sometimes you must do "back seat driving" to get the job done.

55. MICROMANAGEMENT

Mrs. Fernanda was always anxious about her daughter Samantha's education. Samantha was not very bright in her studies. Everyday Mrs. Fernanda would spend many hours with Samantha teaching her, work along with her, and also force her to do plenty of homework. Any mistake was dealt sternly.

When the grades came in, Samantha had not so fancy grades!

Mrs. Fernanda changed her tactics. She thought that her micromanagement was scaring Samantha. Mrs. Fernanda assigned work every morning and Samantha had to show her work at the end of the day.

The grades of Samantha improved. A couple of years later, Mrs. Fernanda stopped managing Samantha's education. Samantha managed her studies well. She turned to be a topper in her class.

Most people hate micromanagement. Micromanagement can backfire.

56. TOE THE LINE

Many years after school, I met my friend Roy. Roy was a brilliant student in our class. After his graduation he became an engineer at a big company. Out of curiosity I asked him why he is not a VP or someone higher up in the executive leadership of the company.

Roy stared at me, He said, "When I was a child my parents were after me. They would ask me to study everyday. If I did not perform well, my parents thought that I brought shame to our family. I studied according to their wishes and followed their dreams. After graduation, I stopped studying, I lost interest in continuing education. I did not want to push my limits. I am happy living my life as an engineer."

I checked my other friends in school who were brilliant in class. Majority of them were burned out. Most of them never rose above their ranks.

Every student should enjoy education. Education should not be boring. It is very difficult for the parents to motivate a child beyond college. The student should have a higher purpose in life and should be self-motivated. The formal education provided by school and college only provides the skeleton. The informal education after graduation should add "flesh."

57. HATE

Everyone around you can understand when you hate your job. Dr. Sabrina came to the US from Central Europe; she eventually found a job at a research laboratory.

One of the duties assigned to Dr. Sabrina was to work on laboratory mice to understand a disease. Every week she had to change the cages of the mice. Dr. Sabrina hated her job.

Dr. Sabrina was always angry handling the mice. She would toss the mice into the new cages from the soiled cage. The mice would run around the cage whenever Dr. Sabrina place her hand in the cage.

Whenever Dr. Sabrina goes for vacation, her colleague, Dr. Nadia would take care of the animals. Dr. Nadia placed the animals gently into the fresh cages. The mice would stay still when Dr. Nadia was around.

The same is true in homes, office, and factories. If a member hates the job, everyone can feel the pulse.

58. FEAR

What happens when you are lazy and do not study or work when you are young? Eventually you doubt yourself. You believe you are not talented. Fear sets in.

You do not fear others, but yourself. You fear your abilities. You fear you will be failing in whatever you do.

Learn everything at a young age if possible. Never lose an opportunity that comes your way. Collaborate with talented people engaged in diverse fields. Take time to read everyday.

59. THE BONE

Some people are so talkative, may be because the tongue does not have a bone!

I had a young talkative colleague, Ms. Amber who came straight to work from college. I always wondered if she even talked during her sleep. Occasionally, I would remind her of her annoying talkative nature, which she would brush aside.

One day during my field trip in the forest I found a bone of an animal on the forest floor. I took it to the Institute. I met Ms. Amber the following day.

"Ms. Amber, I found something you lost."

"What is it?"

I handed the bone to her, "Your tongue bone!"

Ms. Amber never talked too much after the incident.

Sometimes you have to put on a show to make a point.

60. ANERGIC LEADERSHIP

Leaders are not super humans to understand and to react to every incident or needs around them. However, they have experienced advisers giving suggestions and advice on important matters. It is up to the leader to execute or implement decisions in a timely manner based on suggestion of the advisers, his/her gut instincts, education, experience and knowledge.

Anergy is a term in immunology that describes a lack of reaction by the body's immune system to fight foreign substances. Unresponsive or anergic leaders delay decisions to the extent that their slow actions have a negative impact on the well-being of the society they serve. Anergic leaders ignore or are not aware of the need of the society they serve. Anergic leaders have less compassion and empathy to the needs of the society. Anergic leaders also populate leadership positions with unqualified personnel that pay homage and only listen to him. Some of these leaders see everything in the prism of economics. A delayed decision has ramification that extends to several generations.

In many countries the COVID-19 pandemic showed how anergic leadership negatively impacted the society. They downplayed the importance of the pandemic and this led to the flaring of the disease and the deaths associated with it. Lockdowns and cease of economic activities in the early phase of the pandemic would have drastically cut deaths due to COVID-19.

Reference:

Thomas, S. (2022). Status of COVID-19 pandemic before the administration of vaccine. Methods in Molecular Biology 2410: 93-108. (Coined the term: Anergic Leadership for leaders that do not act on advice, suggestion and feedback).

61. IGNORE

Mr. Jacob was the first person to come to his office for work. While he came to the office the cleaning crew would only be halfway through their job.

Mr. Jacob's department had a water filter unit that had to be manually filled. Once Mr. Jacob saw that the filter unit was contaminated. He reported the condition of the filter to the supervisor.

Mr. Jacob's supervisor was lethargic. He did not have any leadership acumen. He said, "I bring water from my house."

Mr. Jacob left a note on the water filter unit. "Contaminated, do not drink water."

*****

After the hurricane, the university buildings were flooded. Most of the water distillation units of our department was badly damaged. We lost many weeks to clean up. It was time to submit our reports; hence, we had to start the laboratory work quickly.

We used the distillation facility of the neighboring department that was operational. I had to lug the big can to the adjacent building.

Once the secretary of the department noticed me lugging the water can. She was shocked to see me carrying the large water can and notified the incident to the chairman of the department.

The chairman said, "Ignore."

Fortunately, the chairman of the department had to go for a medical procedure and an acting chairman was assigned. The secretary stated again the need to fix the distillation unit to the acting chairman.

The acting chairman was sympathetic to the cause. Within a couple of days, the problem was solved, and the distillation unit started functioning.

Do not close your eyes when a genuine request is made.

62. FIRST THEY IGNORE YOU, LATER THEY WILL BE YOUR ADVOCATE

In college, Elizabeth participated in a cooking competition. She decided to try a new variety of *payasam*, a South Indian dessert.

The *payasam* is usually made of rice, wheat, green gram or banana. Elizabeth used pumpkin as the base for her dessert.

The students laughed at Elizabeth when the pumpkin *payasam* was displayed. Later, the judges came and tasted her dessert. They were overjoyed to see and taste a new and original recipe. They asked for more!

After the judges left, Elizabeth's friends and classmates became curious. They tasted her dessert as the judges were happy after the tasting. Within ten minutes her dessert bowl was empty.

Later that day, when the prizes were announced, Elizabeth's *payasam* was a winner.

When you bring out a new product, initially people will ignore you, later they will be your advocate.

63. SHOP LIKE A LOCAL

Joe and his siblings along with his mother moved to the city for schooling. Joe's father was a planter and would only come during the weekend. Joe was the eldest son of the family and was responsible for the family.

It was a different age and time and there were few public transport facilities. Joe had to walk for grocery shopping. Joe initially purchased groceries and produce by weight. He observed the local people shopping; they purchased produce by the amount of money.

The local people would say to the shopkeeper, "I want carrot for Rs. 2.00 or onion for Rs. 3.00." In fact, they would get more produce if purchased by the amount of money than by weight.

Fish and poultry were purchased from the market. Joe understood that the shops at the entrance of the market charged more than the shops inside the market.

As Joe was a bargain shopper, the grocery bill was always less than the anticipated weekly budget.

Years later, Joe completed his studies and moved to Texas. While shopping for a house he understood that the main banks charged more interest compared to cooperative banks and local banks.

Joe negotiated with the manager of the local bank. Joe said, "My budget is $1250.00. Could you find a mortgage at that rate?"

Joe had an excellent credit score, and the manager did not want to let go off a good client. Joe found a mortgage in his budget. The major banks quoted $1500.00 for the same service!

Shop like a local. Observe the business around you.

64. EXPERIENCE

After two years of living in our house, we moved out as we had to relocate to a far-away city for a job. We tried to sell the house. Unfortunately, we could not find any buyer.

We rented the house to a family. Every two months I would receive a call to fix some issue. Years passed....One time I did not receive any complaints for two straight months. I was happy that I did not have to dole out money to fix anything. However, my joy was short lived.

Two days later, hurricane struck. The house was flooded, four feet! The renters moved out in a boat in the middle of the night. The whole city was under flood. It was difficult to find a contractor.

Finally, after googling for one hour I found a contractor. Every evening the contractor would send me the pictures of her work. I could not travel to the house as my job was more than three hours by flight. After eight months of work the house was back in shape. Though I tried to sell it, it was futile.

The house was rented out again, and a family moved in. Eventually I asked if they were interested to buy it. Who else did not wish to buy a brand-new house with new appliances by the side of the bayou! The renter agreed. After the formalities were over, I said goodbye to our first house.

The children were growing up. I needed a house and found one near my job that required repairs. The experience in building our house after the hurricane encouraged me to buy it. I would never had brought the house if I had no prior experience in construction. I fixed the house and moved in within a month.

Everything happens for a purpose.

65. WASTED EDUCATION

A friend once said, "We studied equations, calculus etc., in school. We are not using any of these in our daily lives."

"How old is your child?"

"10 years."

"In another couple of years, you will be teaching your child the same equations and calculus. If you live longer you will also teach your grandchildren."

66. ONE VOICE

Alexander was a strict father. He wished to see his children highly educated. He did not like the children sitting idle or playing with friends.

The children's friends played video games and they also wished to have one. The children begged Alexander to purchase video games for them. Alexander disagreed.

The children nagged their mother, Elina for the video game. Finally Elina gave in. Though Alexander objected, Elina quarreled with him and bought the video game for the children.

The video game had a negative impact on the education of the children. They lost interest in studies. The children received poor grades in their exams.

Elina was worried seeing the poor grades of her children. She requested the children to stop playing video games and concentrate on their studies.

The children shot back, "Mama don't interfere in our games."

Every house should have only one voice.

67. VALUE

At every stages of our life we have to create value for ourselves. When you are a student you create value for yourself by studying well, developing talents in music and arts, computer programming, sports, doing social work, publishing scientific papers and setting up small business. The value that you create when you are a student would lead to a good university where you could study on a full scholarship.

When you are employed, you create value by investing in companies, developing patents, reading journals and bringing new ideas to the table, publishing books and scientific papers, working for non-profit companies, be a consultant for companies, investing in management education, taking care of health and family. The value you create would lead to leadership positions.

When you are retired, you create value by staying healthy and also motivating the society. You create value when you have a healthy diet and also indulge in physical activity like gardening, travelling, working out everyday, and also socializing with family members and maintaining a spiritual life. In addition you create value to the society when you share your experience with others, motivate the society by lectures and books.

The value you create will not only impact you, but also impact your family, the society and your country.

68. EIFFEL TOWER

When the Eiffel tower was built in Paris, many Parisians hated it. With time, people loved the tower design and eventually it became the icon of Paris and of France.

So, why did people change their opinion of the Eiffel tower?

People never changed their opinion of the Eiffel tower. The generation that hated the design of the Eiffel tower died. If you wake up the dead, they will still have the same opinion! The subsequent generations liked the design of the Eiffel tower.

People may hate your product or design or your personality initially. The opinion changes with time. Sometimes your personality may be hated by people in your existing company but may be adored, valued or respected in another company.

69. INSURANCE

A road passed through a public golf course not far from my home. Once driving through that road, I saw many people waiting to cross the road. The crowd was spilling over to the road; it was a dangerous scenario. I slowly stopped my vehicle so that people could cross the road.

As I stopped the vehicle, I heard a sound...WHAM! The driver behind me was on her cell phone and did not notice me stopping my vehicle. My car was badly damaged.

After the police report was filed, the insurance agent came and inspected my vehicle. The impact had damaged the chassis. The car was expensive to be repaired. Hence it was considered totaled.

The insurance agent worked on the numbers after inspecting the car. The car had been with me for seven years. I was given the same amount of money that I had paid seven years back.

I asked the insurance agent how she came up with the numbers. "I checked the condition of your vehicle and how you maintained the vehicle. The vehicle was kept clean."

Our house and our vehicle are not ours; it belongs to the next person who inherit it. Keep it tidy.

During interviews, sometimes the hiring manager will accompany you to your vehicle while leaving. When you enter your vehicle, the hiring manager will inspect your vehicle discreetly. Often, the selection is made on how you take care of your vehicle.

70. THE CEO

One summer I went to my father's estate for the holiday. While at the estate I noticed a young diligent lady taking care of the produce, drying it and packing it.

My father pointed at her and said, "Her parents came here as refugees many years back. One day I saw her mother plucking cloves, her daughter, may be two years old, was lying in the shade. Seeing her physical condition, I knew something was wrong with her. I asked my driver to rush her to the hospital. She was lucky to get to the hospital on time. Eventually she regained health and grew to the hardworking lady you see over there."

***

The laborers in the estate were paid every Saturday. At that time transactions were in hard currency.

In those days, the banks provided soiled currency bills as there was a shortage of clean currency bills. Every weekend my father would visit us in the city. Mondays he would go to the Reserve Bank branch, where my father would trade his old currency bills for new ones. He had to stand long lines to get the new currency bills. He would give the laborers the new currency bills and they were proud to receive the new bills and shiny new coins.

***

Some of the laborers did not care how they dressed when they left the estate for vacation. If my father saw that the laborers were dressed shabbily, he would call them and asked them to change their clothes and put a nice one. His logic was that when his laborers wore shabby dress, people will notice and he will be at fault for not treating his laborers well.

71. THE LEGACY

We are all actors who play our roles and leave the planet once our role is over. Our roles are strong if we know the purpose in our life.

My father's assignment given to him by his parents when he entered the work force was to take care of his employees.

When I was a kid I threw tantrums at an employee. My father saw and was angry at my behavior. "These are my employees, you have no right to treat them badly. I should never see you behaving rudely especially to employees who work for you."

Years passed, my college education was over. My father decided to retire after selling his estate. Usually he does not engage me in any of his business. He took me to see a long time client, to bid farewell. My father's client served us tea, and while having tea he said, "It is sad that you are selling your estate. I am sorry for the employees at the estate. They will never have an employer who treats them with respect." Sometimes in life you see the veil of your legacy closing in front of you. That moment was the "veil moment" of my father. My father's parents were not present to see his final moment of a long career; that role fell on me. He followed the advice of treating his employees with respect till the end of his career, and that was his legacy.

72. SAYING NO

Sometimes in life you have to learn to say no to a request or offer. Most people smoke or drink or gamble for the first time at the request of a friend. They may offer the first cigar or glass of beer or other liquor for free. It might be the start of a bad behavior. If you think you can control your thoughts or cravings, think again. Sometimes it is difficult to get rid of a vice. Do not start one for making someone happy.

When you are successful, there may be many people around you that would like to see you fail. Look out for those people. Say no to their requests or offers. Everyone around you has a hidden agenda. It is better to be lonely at the top than lonely in the ditch later.

73. LUCK

At every success of yours, your colleagues and family think that you are lucky. Luck is not permanent. It may run out at any moment. There are umpteen stories where people became millionaires and died penniless. Majority of the people who became millionaires overnight after winning lottery, squandered it within a couple of years. People who were once healthy would turn sick for months and years. When you are lucky, be it health or wealth, do not abuse your fortune. You can only say if someone was lucky after his/her death.

74. ORGANIZATION

Each of us is an organization. Our education, experience and dreams should lead us forward. Don't rely or trust anyone while moving forward. You cannot rely on your parents, siblings, spouse, children, friends, or colleagues. These individuals may not be there always with you moving forward. If you have a dream, chase your dream; you have to work hard to fulfill it. Sometimes you fail but consider failure as a lesson and move on.

***

The humble grass is small, whereas the majestic giant sequoia trees are large. What makes the grass small, whereas the sequoia trees large – its DNA. People in an organization is its DNA. Large companies are larger and small companies are smaller because of its people and the values they have.

75. MANAGEMENT BOOK

Often, we hate when our employer takes a decision that does not make any sense. If the management decision is not wise according to your concept write them on the left pages of a book. Write the alternate good management decision on the right pages of the book. When you get to be the supervisor or manager, you should implement the good management practices that was written on the right pages of the book.

76. THE SMART PHONE

Several decades back in when the mobile phone was introduced, snobs used to show off their brick shaped phones. The lesser mortals were jealous of the rich kids holding their phones. A couple of years later the telephone carriers introduced the free phone to any subscribers. Immediately, the mobile phone became popular all over the world. People who dreamed of having a mobile phone had access to it. Years later, the smart phone was introduced. People were in awe seeing the smart phones in the hands of their neighbors. Though the telephone companies provided free smart phones initially, they discontinued it later due to high cost of the smart phone. However, as commercial and government organizations had started communicating with people using smart phones, it became an essential equipment. After COVID-19, business and education became online, this increased the smart phone sales globally.

What was once a dream for the common man became as essential tool for everyone within a decade after its release.

All our dreams will be a reality in our life.

77. SERVICE

Each one, teach one. – *African-American Proverb.*

All of us preoccupied with work and family duty. Use at least a small percentage of your time and wealth for the benefit of the society. There are scores of non-profit organizations around you. Be active in those organizations or start one if there aren't any that aligns with your values and mission.

Your talents and services may be helpful to scores of people – in education, small business, housing, food and clothing. Your services may also touch the local flora and fauna if you work with environmental organizations.

At the end, you will be known by the services rendered to the society, not your wealth.

78. DRIVER

What drives you everyday when you wake up? For some people it is the wages earned. For some others it is the power and the respect earned in the society.

Your money or power should not drive you. They are not permanent. In fact, if they drive you, you burn out after some time.

At some point in your life, your world may come crashing on you. Curiosity, passion, a sense of purpose and your mission should drive you everyday.

79. TESTIMONY

Prof. Constantin had hired a technician for his laboratory work. The technician turned out to be a "pain" for the professor due to her unprofessional work ethic. Prof. Constantin was a gentleman; all his previous students were well known scientists and professors. He had never "fired" anyone in his life.

After a year into her job, the technician applied for a job at a bigger organization. She was hired for the job. Everyone around was curious and asked Prof. Constantin how his technician landed the job. The professor replied, "Since I didn't want the technician here anymore, I wrote a very favorable recommendation letter when the organization contacted me."

80. THE LEADER

August 14, 2003: Power outage in Northeast USA. New York City was also not spared. The subway system grinded to a halt. People had to walk home after work. The city was flooded with people. Prof. Peter Palese, the Chairman of Microbiology of Mount Sinai School Medicine went lab to lab asking what he could do to help. He carried with him spare electrical plugs and extension cords to connect equipments to the emergency outlet.

Many of the professors left the building within five minutes of the outage leaving the students in the laboratory. The Hospital had given us thirty minutes to leave the building. Prof. Peter Palese was the last to leave the Department. I was ahead of him. We had to walk down sixteen floors. That was easy, but I had to climb twenty two floors to reach home. The dim light of the cell phone guided me.

81. STORM

Even if you are a sage, you will pass through storms in your life. Doesn't matter how good you are, what good works you have done to the society, there will be a day where you will be tested. Most probably, you will be alone. The friends and family surrounding you will be nowhere near. Do not wobble. Stay with your Creator, pray, be at peace. Live by your faith.

If the Lord brings you to it, He will take you through it. Every storm will pass. After a while, the clouds will vanish, and you will come out more glorious than ever.

82. THE MEEK ALSO WIELDS POWER

One summer, Philip went for a ride to the countryside. Returning, he had to pass through an unmanned toll gate. An exact toll of 50 cents (two quarters) was required to open the unmanned toll gate. Unfortunately, Philip did not have any quarters with him. His purse contained several one hundred, twenty, five and one dollar bills; in addition he had his credit card worth twenty thousand dollars. Philip felt frustrated and powerless as his money was of no use at that moment. The large denominations of his money could not open the toll gate. He backed up his car and waited for a traveler to pass by. Luckily, after 10 minutes of wait, a car came to a halt in front of the toll gate. Philip reached out to the passenger and exchanged his one-dollar bill for the quarters.

In your life, you might have very rich and powerful friends. Sometimes the 'not so rich and powerful friend' may be the one to help you at a crucial moment.

83. FLAVORS OF MONEY

When running a non-profit organization, money is required to run the programs of organization. Often you will have to do fundraising to run the activities of the organization.

Money comes in "different flavors". Most people are honest and make money by working hard. Some people cheat to make money; whereas some others may indulge in illicit or illegal trading to make money. Even among the hardworking folks, there may be misers who do not like to partake any money for the public good. It is better not to ask money from misers or people engaged in illicit trading for your nonprofit organization.

84. GLORY DAYS

Mr. George had a fine taste. He lived in a splendid house that was meticulously taken care of by his employees. The house had exotic plants and a beautiful garden. One day Mr. George suddenly died. Mrs. George and eventually the children had to take care of the house. The house was just a shadow of its former glory.

Some organizations are managed well by good administrators. However, when the administrator leaves, no matter who is in charge, the organization do not regain the past glory.

85. AWARD

The department put out a request before Christmas to nominate colleagues for the "best person of the year" based on work culture and overall personality. Every person was issued a blank card to fill in the nomination.

I nominated a couple of colleagues for the award. Everyone in my group threw the nomination card in the garbage box. The colleagues I nominated won the award.

People criticize for the smallest mistake. Whereas, it is difficult to get a commendation from colleagues even when you do something good.

86. CONTINUING EDUCATION

Most people throw their books once the exams of the terminal degree are over. The education imparted at the college or university only provides a 'skeleton' of information. You have to put in 'muscle' by reading more books and technical papers. Whatever you learned in college will be obsolete in ten years after completion of your education. Thus, there is a need to update your knowledge continuously.

A few decades back one had to go to the library to read. Currently every information is available in your phone or computer. All you need is find time to read. You have to prioritize what you want in life – entertainment or knowledge.

Due to advances in medicine and technology, people are living longer than the previous generation. We do not know the future economic situation. Within a few years, oil will be phased out, thereby lowering the tax revenues. It is difficult to predict the future economic situation.

To stay relevant, one must educate on a daily basis. By default, after ten years of work, most people are managers leading a team. Even if you do not have the title of a manager, you will be having a subordinate or assistant that you have to lead. You may be technically brilliant, but a poor manager. To be a good manager one has to read management books early in life. Your IQ (intelligent quotient) and EQ (emotional quotient) should merge to be a great manager.

The challenges faced by the future generation includes climate change and automation. Climate change will impact the food security, health and the economy. The current jobs, whatever we see around, will be negatively influenced by automation. Automation will also give rise to new jobs. Hence, continuing education is essential to move ahead.

87. PATIENCE

Every summer I take the children for fishing in the nearby lake. You learn patience while fishing.

The children are happy to go fishing. They run to the backyard to collect earthworms to be used as bait.

The children have a poor catch when they start late in the afternoon. However, one hour before the sun goes down the weather changes. The light wind turns the water cooler. Once the temperature of the water drops there is a spike in the fish catch. The children are thrilled when the fish catch goes up. They do not want to leave the lake. Once it gets dark, the park rangers shout through PA system to leave, and the children wind their lines. Sometimes, the children find fish caught in the hook while winding the fishing line!

Everyone has dreams in their life. Some people plot their life to get rich quickly. They get rich quickly and eventually lose everything quickly! Be patient with your dreams; you will accomplish whatever you dreamed.

88. WISH

During the last day of the tenth grade, one of our teacher asked the class what they wished to be. Every student stated their career of interest that they would like to pursue. The students chased their dreams.

Ten years later, everyone in the class became what they wished to be.

In my laboratory, I train students of the neighboring university. While interviewing, I ask them what career they would like to pursue. Some of the students have no idea what career they would like to pursue in spite of spending $ 200,000 for their graduate education! I usually reject those students as it is not worth training them.

Dare to dream.

89. SEEING THE EMPLOYER IN THE EYES OF AN EMPLOYEE

Once while driving, the pressure warning light of the dashboard lit up. I took the car to the nearby automobile workshop. The workshop was very clean and tidy. I spoke to the clerk about my situation. His face looked nervous. He asked me to speak to the owner. I saw the nervousness on the face of all the employees while walking towards the owner.

The owner had no smile on his face. He asked, "Do you have an appointment?"

I said, "No. This is an emergency."

The owner shot back, "Come back after you schedule an appointment."

While walking back to my car I stated jokingly, "The tire did not schedule an appointment with me before getting punctured by a nail."

I drove to my regular automobile workshop down the road. The workshop was not very tidy. The owner and the staff were friendly. They would always greet me and fix any problems within minutes. Immediately on arrival, the owner asked the technician to take care of my vehicle. He found a nail on the tire. He removed it and plugged it.

"This is a new tire. This tire could go for several hundred miles, just keep an eye on the tire."

I asked, "How much did it cost for servicing the tire?"

"Nothing."

You can sense the personality of an employer in the eyes of the employee.

90. THE INTERVIEW

Organizations interview people to select the suitable candidates for the job. They also look for the values of the candidates and see if they are a right fit for the organization and also for the people working there.

Organizations look for talented candidates that are better than existing employees; they also look for candidates who are easily trainable.

Interview is a drama. Some candidates act very well; it is difficult to understand the original behavior of the candidate.

If interviews are done at a formal dining table it is difficult to act while dining. If you pay attention you can understand the real behavior of the candidate.

91. VALUES

Does your values and philosophy help you succeed in life.

Success doesn't mean getting a huge salary or having power and position. It means more than that. If you have touched someone's life or if your work has impacted the society, you have succeeded in your mission.

Do not be awe struck by people that are rich and famous and try to emulate them. You do not know how they succeeded or the path they followed to succeed in life. Society always values glamour and power. Success may not be genuine; failure is genuine.

Hold on to your values. Let your values lead you in life. If you have put a smile on someone, you have succeeded in life.

92. CHANCE FAVORS THE PREPARED MIND

Stamp collection (philately) is a hobby of children and adults. Every year postal organizations brings out new stamps on varied subjects. Postal organizations check for errors before the stamps are delivered. If any error is found they remove the stamps before circulation. Once in a while, error stamps goes into circulation. However, as they are of minimum number, they later command huge prices at the auction house (eg. Inverted Jenny).

In December 2010, the United States Postal Service (USPS) released the Lady Liberty Forever stamp. The USPS printed billions of stamps (10.5 billion).

In early 2011, while working at the University of Texas Medical Branch, I observed an envelope franked with the new Lady Liberty stamp lying in the copy room.

WHAT!!!!....I shouted.

Many months before the incident, while working in the category "Statue of Liberty" for Sunipix, the independent stock photo agency, I wished to know the difference between the Lady Liberty in New York and its small replica in Las Vegas (in front of the New York, New York Casino). A quick glance at the images from Google helped me identify the differences.

Unfortunately, the Lady Liberty depicted in the Forever stamp was the replica at Las Vegas, not the original Lady Liberty statue at New York.

I immediately contacted the Director General of USPS. I send him the original Lady Liberty images posted at Sunipix as reference. There was a frantic search at USPS and the next day they admitted it was an error in their part. Meanwhile, I also did my research and found that the USPS obtained the image from Getty images, the world's largest photo stock agency. It was clearly stated that the Lady Liberty was the Las Vegas replica. Looked like someone at USPS didn't read the fine print.

The Lady Liberty Forever stamp is the largest error on a postage stamp.

Twist: Months later, the sculptor of the replica at Las Vegas sued USPS. He claimed he modelled the Lady Liberty at Las Vegas based on the face of his mother-in-law!! He won the case. USPS payed $3.5 million to the sculptor of the Lady Liberty replica at Las Vegas.

93. COLLABORATION

When you work alone, your actions have limits. If you collaborate, there are infinite opportunities.

A few years back I wished to write a review paper on the microbiome. I used to write the paper after my laboratory work. A couple of months later, seeing the pace of my writing I understood that the paper will never get anywhere. I immediately wrote the heading of different subsections and searched for people who had worked in those areas. I wrote a good cover letter enticing people the need for collaborating on a microbiome review paper.

All I requested from the authors was around 2000 words on a particular topic. One month later I received the sections from the authors. When I wished to have an illustration for the paper, a collaborator reached out to her collaborator and made several illustrations.

The reviewers and editors were not happy seeing a lengthy review paper. Most journals publish reviews that are only 5-10 pages. Our paper was 30 pages!! I stated to the editor that reducing the page length will impact the quality of the paper.

The journal agreed to publish the review. The paper: The Host Microbiome Regulates and

Maintains Human Health: A Primer and Perspective for Non-Microbiologists. Cancer Research (2017) 77(8):1783-1812, is highly popular since its publication.

Often times in our life, business or career will be stagnant. If so, reach out and find a collaborator to improve your business.

94. ONE DOLLAR, BOEING 747, ST. GEORGE AND COVID-19

December 15, 2019: The COVID-19 disease was first reported in China. Eventually, the disease spread throughout the world. The disease caused by SARS-CoV-2 was anything the world had seen before in the recent memory.

Researchers rushed to study the virus and develop a vaccine. Everyone was racing against time to get information on the virus. SARS-CoV-2 is a coronavirus with Spike (S), Membrane (M), Envelope (E) and Nucleocapsid (N) proteins. As the S protein is involved in binding to the human cell receptor people rushed to study the protein. Everyone was chasing S......; it was a rat race out there.

I was also interested in developing a vaccine candidate. You need resources to develop a project. In April 22, a grant slipped by. I looked outside the window...what next... (Everyone must have faced such moments in life).

I went home and started working on the SARS-CoV-2 proteins in the computer. Due to the availability of free bioinformatics software, currently one can do plenty of work *in silico*. While working on the M protein, the software predicted it as a sugar transporter. I quickly searched the literature- no one had reported that the M protein, the largest SARS-CoV-2 protein has a sugar transporter like structure. Unfortunately, I did not have much protein modelling experience. The country was in a partial lockdown and it was difficult to find investigators to do the modelling work of the protein.

Nearly, two decades back while walking on the streets of New York City I came in front of the Strand Book Store, the largest used book store in the world. Outside the book store was a book on the Boeing Company that was marked for One dollar. The book stated how the company struggled to build the Boeing 747. It was their largest venture. It needed huge infrastructure. Due to lack of time, they build the airplane and the factory simultaneously.

I followed the same Boeing model. I studied protein modelling and wrote the paper simultaneously on April 23, St. George day.

"And I will ask the Father, and he will give you another advocate to help you and be with you forever." John 14:16.

I called my "advocate" to help me. We worked on the protein models and wrote the paper together. Three days later I completed writing the paper (the fastest paper ever written by me). I submitted it to Preprints, the preprint server and they accepted it after a couple of days. Later, the article was published in a journal: The

Structure of the Membrane Protein of SARS-CoV-2 Resembles the Sugar Transporter SemiSWEET. Pathogens and Immunity (2020) 5(1):342-363.

The paper was well received.

Tail piece: Couple of months after publishing the paper, the Boeing Company stated that they are discontinuing production of the Boeing 747!!!

Some of the innovations that helped humanity overcome COVID-19: Preprint servers (the idea of using mask to prevent infection was published in Preprints), e-commerce (delivery to home), and video meeting.

Do not be afraid to learn new things. Your life begins at the end of the comfort zone. Sometimes you may not have anyone to help you in your projects. Your prayer works miracles. Believe.

95. MORTGAGE

Refinancing a mortgage requires large amount of money. Sometime back, I was running from door-to-door to get a good deal in refinancing our mortgage. Every bank stated that I need to bring in plenty of cash for the closing. The officer of our bank stated, "It is not worth refinancing with your budget."

Several months passed, I went to a bank branch near my office to pay the mortgage. I prayed, "God, show me a way to refinance the house cheaply."

Just as I was paying the mortgage, an officer of the bank came to speak to the teller. She looked at my mortgage statement and said, "I want to speak to you. Can you come to my office?"

"Of course."

I walked into her office. The officer said, "We have good refinancing deals. Are you interested?"

"Does it involve any closing costs?"

"None."

I was happy. She took all my details and a couple of weeks later my mortgage was refinanced. I paid a lower interest rate.

Prayer works. Ask and it shall be given to you (Matthew 7:7).

96. GIVE US THIS DAY OUR DAILY BREAD

As a family of faith, we daily pray the Lord's Prayer: Our Father, who art in heaven, hallowed be thy name; thy kingdom come; thy will be done on earth as it is in heaven. Give us this day our daily bread; and forgive us our trespasses as we forgive those who trespass against us; and lead us not into temptation, but deliver us from evil. Amen.

I did my research at an Institute in a rural area. We used to get breakfast and lunch at the Institute, but not dinner. There were only a few grocery stores and restaurants in the small village. Most of them used to close around 8:00PM.

My research days were longer. I started around 8:30 AM and work ended around 10:00 PM. The last bus to reach home was at 10:00 PM. There was a restaurant at the last bus stop; mainly catering to the tourists and bus employees. The restaurant closed its business around 10:15 PM.

I was living in a house near the last bus stop. The house had minimum facilities and no appliances were allowed. Unfortunately, there was also "water curfew" in that area; the water was turned down at 8:00 PM. I used to store water in cans for emergency purposes.

As my days were busy, I was tired, and I hated cooking at night. I had dinner at the restaurant at the last bus stop.

Several days I have missed the bus, or the bus didn't show up due to mechanical failure. On those days I had to walk 30 minutes to reach my house. To my surprise, while walking I would see some restaurants or grocery stores open.

After buying food, I usually ask why they are open at that hour. The stores would say that they had to take care of the accounts or had to stock the shelves.

One day none of the stores and restaurants were open after I missed the last bus. I thought that I had to go to bed on and empty stomach. When I reached home to my surprise there was water in the tap. I cooked food and had dinner.

Your Creator knows what you want. He will provide.

97. THE RETAINING WALL

During monsoon season the river that runs in front of our house cause destruction to the riverbank. To build a river retaining wall was expensive. The local government also had no funds to help us.

My father was always sad during monsoon season seeing the destruction of his property during monsoon. He prayed for a miracle to settle the issue.

One summer someone knocked on his door. It was a contractor asking permission to use his property as a base to build a retaining wall for our neighbor across the river. Many years back the neighbor used his influence to get permission to build a retaining wall for his property. The government at that time had a scheme to construct retaining walls for riverbank. My father was away, and he did not know of the scheme.

My father gave permission to use his property as a base to unload the stones for the work. Several weeks later the contractor returned. He said, "The family across your house leased his land for agriculture purposes. The lessee is unwilling to permit us constructing the retaining wall. We have to complete our work this season or we will lose the funds. May I know if we could construct the retaining wall at your property?"

"Of course, go ahead."

Within a couple of months, the work was over. My father was happy that his prayers were answered.

Believe. Miracles happens with your prayers.

98. ROAD TO SIBERIA

During my post graduate studies, we used industrial alcohol in the laboratory for experimental purposes. The industrial alcohol was delivered in drums in the storage room of the Department. We had to complete several forms and specify the amount of alcohol required for laboratory purposes.

One time I was assigned to get the alcohol for the laboratory. I completed the forms with a request for four liters of alcohol. As I didn't want to go to the storage room every time, I took an additional one liter of alcohol. I placed the bottles in the laboratory and went for lunch.

My hostel, Siberia, was at the far-end of the University. I was walking alone to the hostel; there was no one on the road. Half-way through the hostel, I heard a clear voice, "You only requested four liters of alcohol. You took an additional one liter. Return it back."

Immediately after lunch, I went to the laboratory, took the extra one liter of industrial alcohol, and returned to the storage room.

If I go up to the heavens, you are there; if I make my bed in the depths, you are there. - Psalm 139:8

99. START YOUR DAY WITH A PRAYER, END YOUR DAY WITH A PRAYER

One summer, a high school student came for an internship in my laboratory. The student was close to the family of my professor. The student was not very passionate; she just did what I said. Any assignment given to her was done in a hurry before coming to the laboratory. She also didn't take any initiative to do any experiments.

I always start a day with a prayer and end the day with a prayer. It is not our abilities that lead us.

One day I said to my student, "Start the day with a prayer when you start working in the laboratory and end the day with a prayer before leaving."

A couple of days later, the professor came to me. He was furious. He said, "Why did you tell the student to pray before working. She is from an atheist family."

I didn't reply or apologize. I stood my ground.

I forgot the matter and moved on. A few months later, I was in the conference hall of the Medical School attending a seminar series. The hall was almost full. Towards the middle of the seminar, I heard a clear voice, "Your professor will lose his job."

I knew that if my professor leave, I will be toast. A few weeks later the professor was scrutinized for scientific integrity. Some of the data published many years back, prior to my work in the laboratory were questioned by the authorities.

One time, the committee called me and asked my opinion of the professor. I used all the superlatives to praise my professor. At the end of the meeting, I thought that since I had a high opinion about the professor, he will be safe.

Months passed; the laboratory was busy with experiments. The city was getting ready for Easter.

I do not work on Good Friday since it is a day of obligation. When I came back after Easter, I saw a note on my desk from the professor, "I am leaving, take care of the laboratory."

After a few months, several of the professor's papers that was published many years earlier were retracted from scientific journals.

Whoever acknowledges me before others, I will also acknowledge before my Father in heaven. But whoever disowns me before others, I will disown before my Father in heaven. – Matthew 10:32-33.

100. THE SOUL

What is man? Man is body, soul and Spirit.

Friday 19 July, 1991, cousin Tony came to the city for business. That night he stayed with us. The "official rule" in our house was that when a guest stays in our house, I had no access to my bed and had to sleep on the sofa in the living room. Since Saturday was a holiday I had to do the shopping. Morning I had to get the milk from the kiosk nearby and later after breakfast I had to do grocery shopping in the center city.

During my student days, I was the first person to wake up in our home. I used to wake up before 5:00 AM and start my studies; all others in our house would wake up at 5:30 AM. No one was allowed to stay in bed after 5:30 AM.

Friday night we had a chat with Tony and all of us went to bed around 10:30 PM; the small lamp in the dining room was turned on as usual before going to bed.

In the early hours of Saturday, I heard a knock on the door and someone opening the door. I opened my eyes and wished to know who woke up earlier. I saw no one; however, a few seconds later I saw a gray colored humanoid approaching my sofa. I was really afraid. I had read about souls in books; but this was the first time I saw one. The soul just passed by me. I

164

said all the prayers that I could remember and closed my eyes.

Every morning the newspaper was delivered at 6:00 AM, but on Saturday July 20, 1991 the newspaper was late. I wondered why the newspaper was late. As scheduled, I went to get the milk from the kiosk. Unfortunately, there was no milk in the nearest kiosk. I knew all the kiosks nearby, so I walked to the neighboring kiosk. Same scenario, no milk. The last kiosk in the area was near the palace gate; luckily I got milk from that kiosk.

The newspaper was delivered before breakfast. The headline was that the Maharaja Sri Chithira Thirunal Balarama Varma, the last king of Travancore passed away early morning. Though we lived within a kilometer, we never crossed paths. I had only seen the Maharaja on television.

After breakfast, Cousin Tony left for business. Since the Maharaja was a major personality in Travancore history, I took my brother to the State Secretariat where his body was kept for the public to pay homage.

That afternoon during lunch at the dining table I said what I saw at night. Everyone was afraid and stared at me.

Around 4:00 PM Tony arrived after successfully completing his business. Since he was leaving for his home, I took him to the bus stop. While waiting at the bus stop the hearse of the Maharaja passed by slowly.

Years passed. While working for my Ph.D, I was assigned a unit (housing) in a labor lines near a dam reservoir that was 15 minutes from the Institute. When I was assigned housing, there was no one living in any of the units. The labor lines were old and must have been built during the dam construction.

I always wondered why the housing was empty. Later, I heard that there was no one living in those housing because someone died of unnatural causes long time back.

The housing unit that was assigned was in a bad shape. I asked a handyman to fix it. Since he did not show up I did it myself. I filled in hundreds of holes on the wall left by former tenants and painted the house.

One night while sleeping, I saw a formless structure about to enter me. The prayers went up in my mind, a bright light appeared and the formless structure fled. Several nights later the same thing repeated; when the bright light appeared, the formless structure disappeared.

One night when the same thing happened, I opened my eyes. I saw a transparent humanoid sitting and praying. Its torso and head were outside me, the leg was inside me. I recognized it as my soul. If my soul was outside my body, I would have died.

There are three entities in a human. The body that is influenced by all the physical forces in the universe; the soul that is not influenced by any physical forces; and the Spirit of our Creator that guides us. The Holy Spirit will only be in you if you call him. The soul's destiny is influenced by your actions.

Every human has an expiry date. However, your soul is eternal. Never lose your soul.

www.ingramcontent.com/pod-product-compliance
Lightning Source LLC
Chambersburg PA
CBHW071220090426
42736CB00014B/2904